MEDIEVAL EARTHWORK SOUTH-WEST LEICESTER

HINCKLEY & BOSWORTH

By
Robert F Hartley

Edited by
Kathleen E Elkin

This volume is dedicated to the memory of
James Pickering AFC, AE, FGS, FSA
(1915-2004)

Jim was a proud son of Hinckley, with a keen interest in local history and archaeology.
In wartime he served his country as a pilot in the RAF.

In peacetime he surveyed his country from the air and recorded hundreds of
archaeological sites, many of which might otherwise never have been known.

The author had the privilege of accompanying him on many of these flights, between
1979 and 1995.

Leicestershire Museums Archaeological Fieldwork Group
(LMAFG)
Monograph No. 2
2008

Acknowledgements

This volume has been sponsored by the Leicestershire Museums Archaeological Fieldwork Group (LMAFG). It is the latest in a series that originally began publication in the 1980s under the auspices of then Leicestershire Museums, Arts and Records Service.

LMAFG would like to thank Alan Chapman, Sandie Smith, and staff in the Highways, Transportation and Waste Department for scanning the originals of the large scale plans drawn up by the author. The method of preparation of this volume has changed greatly since the first one appeared. Then, they were typed and put together by hand. The advent of computers and digital imaging has meant that this has been done entirely using software for digital manipulation of drawings and text. It is hoped that additional volumes in the series will also be produced in future years.

The author would like to acknowledge the assistance of Bob Rutland, Peter Liddle, Anne Graf and Richard Knox of the County's archaeological staff, and the work of amateur fieldworkers, especially Mick Harding and the late Arthur Hurst.

The editor would like to thank Peter Liddle and Tony Squires for reading the original text and providing comment and suggestions and the Print Unit at County Hall for all their help.

Note on Abbreviations

LCC HER   Heritage and Environment Record, kept at Leicestershire County Council

HBSMR   Historic Buildings, Sites and Monuments Record, a database kept by Leicestershire County Council.

Nichols, 1811, pp XXX. These volumes 1 to 4, each with two parts, were published in the early nineteenth century by John Nichols, antiquarian. They are an unrivalled and rich source of information. Many of his illustrations are used again here. A facsimile copy of the volumes was re-published by Leicestershire County Council in association with S R Publications in 1971. This edition is now out of print and copyright although copies can be viewed at Leicestershire Libraries local studies collections in larger libraries in the county and at the Record Office. The volume relating to the Borough of Hinckley and Bosworth is Volume 4, Part 2, Sparkenhoe Hundred and was published in 1811. The majority of the non-map illustrations are taken from this volume and are therefore not individually referenced. They can be found by looking up the parish/site name in Volume 4 Part 2.

ROLLR   Record Office for Leicester, Leicestershire and Rutland. The Record Office is located in Long Street, Wigston Magna, LE18 2AH. The additional reference given relates to the location of the document within the archive.

TLAHS Transactions of the Leicestershire Archaeological and Historical Society. Volume numbers have been rendered into decimal from their original Roman numbering as per the current Transaction publications of the Society. This also the method used in the indispensable 'Cumulative Index Volumes 21 – 74 (1940-2000)' compiled by Auriol Griffith-Jones and published by the Society in 2005.

ULAS University of Leicester Archaeological Services. Based at Leicester University ULAS is the contract excavation side of the Archaeology and Ancient History Department. ULAS investigates potential archaeological sites in Leicester City, Leicestershire and beyond.

James Pickering

James (Jim) Pickering made an unrivalled contribution to our understanding of Leicestershire's archaeology, by using some of the skills he had learned as a fighter pilot to study the landscape from the air. He carried out hundreds of hours of reconnaissance over the Midlands, and took tens of thousands of photographs, which he then made freely available to national and local archaeologists. His work was recognised by the presentation of a Silver Trowel at the 1986 British Archaeological Awards.

Jim was born on June 4th 1915 into a Hinckley family and was educated at the Wyggeston Boys School in Leicester. He was destined to take over the family printing firm, and it is characteristic that on finishing school he went on to study the business in Germany where the most modern technology was being introduced. He stayed in Dresden and absorbed something of the intellectual culture of that place and time; he also visited the 1936 Olympics in Berlin. His time in Germany was pleasant, and he made life-long friends there, but he recognised that the underlying evil of Nazism made war inevitable. On his return to England he joined the RAF Volunteer Reserve.

At weekends he learned to fly Tiger Moths at Desford Aerodrome and then progressed to more modern aircraft. He earned his "wings" as a Sergeant Pilot in April 1939. Although he was one of "The Few" he was destined to miss most of the Battle of Britain, instead he and his Hurricane were sent on convoy to the Mediterranean to reinforce the beleaguered island of Malta. This did nothing to improve his chances of survival; as for the next eight months he and his dwindling band of compatriots flew sorties against overwhelming numbers of enemy aircraft. Jim was the last survivor of the pilots who flew the Gladiator Biplanes "Faith, Hope and Charity", but he was always self-deprecating about his part in this famous episode of warfare.

Eventually getting the chance to leave Malta, he was almost immediately in more trouble – flying into Athens just before it fell to the Nazis. After another lucky escape he became one of a select group of pilots who delivered aircraft to the Middle East and Far East theatres of war. New planes were assembled at Takoradi on the Gold Coast and flown across the jungles and deserts of Africa to Egypt. This was outback aviation, and survival depended on rigorous planning and precise navigation. On one occasion Jim took the opportunity to deliver an aircraft much further along the line, flying over the Himalayas to the American Volunteer Force in China – very much a pioneering achievement at that time.

In late 1942 Jim joined the Western Desert Air Force, and for a while in the spring of 1943 he was flying a captured Italian bomber delivering men and equipment to the front. It is testament to his abilities that he was able to supervise the overhaul of this machine, and write a set of flying instructions for it, starting from first principles!

In June 1943 he returned to Britain and a new role as a test pilot on Spitfires and Mustangs, which gave him an unrivalled knowledge of the landscape as he flew sortie after sortie over the length and breadth of the country. Later, after D-Day, he returned to the fray in France, Belgium and Germany. His experiences as a pilot shaped his work as an aerial archaeologist. It was not just the hours spent in the air, but the variety of flying and the remarkable amount of independence and individual responsibility that he was able to exercise.

After the war Jim was fully involved in business, specialising in printed packaging. He kept his Pilot's licence current and did much flying for the RAF Reserve, training students at Newton near Nottingham and on summer camps elsewhere. At times he had his own aeroplane, including a spell flying the amazing Wallis Autogyro. He had long had an interest in archaeology – his uncle Arthur was Leicestershire's first prominent prehistorian – and he began to photograph sites and correspond with other interested practitioners – notably Derrick Riley and Arnold Baker. For many years he had a villa in Cyprus, and was involved in measures to conserve that island's rich archaeological heritage.

Owing to the success of his business he was able to retire early and concentrate on the search for cropmarks. During the months of June, July and August he would fly as soon as conditions were suitable, and nothing was allowed to take precedence over this work. The hot, dry summer of 1976 in particular saw him clock up over a hundred hours in the air as cropmarks appeared in ripening cereal fields all across the country.

I first met Jim in 1979 when I had just been appointed to the post of Assistant Archaeological Survey Officer for Leicestershire and he offered to take me on a flight to see cropmarks at first hand. Between then and 1996 I was privileged to go along on many flights each year. It was part of Jim's creed that once in the air , if conditions were good one should make as much use of the day as possible, so these flights could cover a lot of country. We ranged from Flamborough Head to Ross on Wye, Northampton to Tadcaster, Shrewsbury to Skegness, taking up to three hundred photographs on a flight, interspersing cross-country transfers with sudden flurries of photography, during which we would descend in orbit after orbit to get the best views.

We would spend perhaps four hours in the air before arriving back at Leicester – invariably on time. Another of Jim's skills was his ability to time a flight, assessing the variables of wind and weather in a way that seemed almost magical. Safely down, we would head for the bar and three or four glasses of Scotch well diluted with water. Even in his late 70s he had remarkable stamina and enthusiasm, and for several summers went as a guest of Otto Braasch to Germany and Hungary, flying long sorties across newly accessible parts of central Europe.

His research project went on for the best part of forty years and its legacy is a huge amount of information, chiefly about Prehistoric England. In 1986 I published with him a summary of known cropmark sites in Leicestershire (Past Worlds in a Landscape – Archaeological Cropmarks in Leicestershire and Rutland, 1986, by James Pickering and Robert F Hartley, Leicestershire Museums) by which time Jim had found and recorded 190 sites, compared with a total of less than 50 found by all other practitioners. In total over 200 sites were found by Jim that would otherwise probably never have been recorded. To this figure should be added hundreds more from twelve other adjoining counties.

Jim went on to become, as he put it, an "Unidentified Flying Octogenarian" before making his last flight in 1998. Typically, he made the decision to ground himself, giving up his Pilot's Licence in 2000.

After a lifetime of action and adventure he did not adapt happily to being a housebound pensioner, but he continued to study his air photo collections and reply to a wide range of correspondents on the subject. He contributed memoirs to several books on wartime flying, as well as attending a number of ceremonial gatherings of wartime fighter pilots.

He freely admitted that the war had given him remarkable experience, and he allied this with his own intellectual gifts and his own money in the service of archaeology. Some people found his brusqueness rude, but he was unfailingly generous with his time and material to those who had a genuine interest in the pursuit of knowledge.

Robert F Hartley 2005

CONTENTS

INTRODUCTION

This is a survey of archaeological evidence revealed by earthwork remains in the area of the present Borough of Hinckley and Bosworth. The evidence is mainly of farming systems and settlements of the period 1000 – 1500 AD, and landscape gardens of the period 1500-1750 AD.

The evidence is drawn mainly from two sources, the first being vertical photographs taken by the RAF in the 1940s and by other organisations in more recent years, and the second being field surveys by the author, carried out mainly in the 1980s.

Hinckley and Bosworth Borough comprises most of the former Hundred of Sparkenhoe. The landscape is in the main a gently undulating plain of clay land with patches of gravels, and there are no major relief features, although at its north-eastern extremities it includes parts of the low granite hills of Charnwood.

In medieval times the area was in the main a typical piece of midland landscape, with evenly spaced nucleated villages surrounded by open-field arable cultivation systems. The material evidence of the open-field systems survived in the form of ridge and furrow earthworks long after its conversion to pasture land, and wide areas of ridge and furrow are clearly recorded on RAF vertical photographs taken in 1948. Almost all of it has, however, been levelled by the plough since the end of the Second World War.

The process of conversion from communal arable farming to separate enclosed pastoral farming took place in Leicestershire in a piecemeal fashion between the 15th and 19th centuries. Alongside this change, and perhaps partly caused by it, there was a change of settlement patterns. Some villages became deserted, either by gradual loss of people, or by the deliberate act of one or more major landholders. In places there was large-scale landscaping to form amenity parks around a new generation of mansion houses.

Almost every village in the area has some evidence of abandoned cottages or farmstead sites recorded in the form of earthworks. The abandonment process continued into the 19th century, when mid-century Tithe Maps often mark the location of dwellings that have not survived to the present. In the second half of the 20th century the process has been reversed as towns have expanded and people have moved out to the villages and travel to work by car. The planning laws of the last half-century have tended to favour new development which "infills" parts of existing villages rather than starting on completely new sites.

Influences on Settlement Pattern
There were in medieval times three major influences on the area that modified parts of the settlement pattern from the prevailing norm. These were 1) the thin-soiled areas of Charnwood, 2) the establishment of the hunting chase and later royal forest known as Leicester Forest, and 3) the slow creation of the extensive landholdings of the Abbey of Merevale.

1) Charnwood
The villages of Stanton under Bardon, Markfield and Groby lie on the edge of the former open common or waste of Charnwood. In the early medieval period parts of this common were gradually being enclosed as assarts and used for woodland, arable land or enclosed pastures. Quite a lot of common land survived in the area

until the final enclosure of Charnwood in the early 1800s.(Crocker J, 1981, Hartley R F, 1989 pp 6-13).

2) Leicester Forest

The heavy clay land between Leicester and Earl Shilton was largely wooded at the time of the Norman Conquest, being used in part to supply firewood and building timber to the town of Leicester. In 1086 the "Hereswode" occupied this area. The name has been interpreted as meaning the "Wood of the Army" or perhaps the "People's Wood". In essence it was the area that provided the town of Leicester with timber for house building and with firewood and certain amount of grazing. After about 1100 successive Earls of Leicester used it as a hunting chase and imposed Forest Laws on the area. They defined a limited area, called The Frith, in which the townsfolk were able to continue to exercise their traditional rights. During the 12th century the Earls allowed the enclosure of land around the forest edge to create pasture land and/or deer parks.

In 1399 it became a royal forest under Henry IV. A boundary to the forest area was established, and access was permitted only along certain routes. The villages of Peckleton and Desford were on the margins of the forest, and the deer parks of Tooley Park, Earl Shilton, and Barn Park, Desford, were created in the former open forest area during the Medieval period. The estates of the Earls of Leicester became part of Duchy of Lancaster, and thence part of the Crown estates in 1399.

A survey in 1523 described the Forest as "a fair and goodly ground, well replenished with deer", but the King's woods were "all decayed and wasted" with few large trees remaining.

King James I and Prince Henry, his eldest son, came to hunt in the Forest in 1612, but by 1628 King Charles I was deeply in debt and the remnant of the Forest was sold off for some £7,000 (Fox L & Russell P, 1948, Leicester Forest, Leicester). The land was subsequently enclosed and farmed.

3) The Lands of Merevale Abbey

Founded by Earl Ferrers in 1148, the Cistercian Abbey of Merevale was endowed with lands by various benefactors, mainly in an area extending across the Leicestershire - Warwickshire border. In southwest Leicestershire the Abbey had estates at Orton on the Hill, Twycross, Sheepy Magna, Sheepy Parva and Ratcliffe Culey. Several of these landholdings were formed into grange farms at Newhouse Grange and Pinwall Grange in Sheepy Magna, Moorbarn Grange on the site of the village of Weston (Twycross), and Lea Grange at Orton on the Hill. (Bloxham M H, 1870, Victoria County History of Warwickshire, pp 75-78).

The only place that still gives us a feeling for the wealth and importance of Merevale Abbey is the magnificent Tithe Barn at Newhouse Grange in Sheepy Magna. There is also a surviving gate chapel on the site with its stained glass that goes some way to showing the wealth and importance of the Abbey. The lands and buildings of Merevale Abbey were surrendered to the King in 1539, when life pensions were granted to the abbot, sub-prior, and eight monks. The site and many of the lands were granted in 1541 to Sir Walter Devereux, Lord Ferrers of Chartley. All that otherwise remains of the Abbey are some substantial ruins built into farm buildings and earthworks.

GAZETTEER OF SITES

The sites are listed under their Civil Parish as defined on the First Edition Ordnance Survey maps of about 1884. In the local government reorganisation of the 1970s many of the Hinckley & Bosworth parishes were amalgamated, but the older boundaries are more useful for an understanding of the medieval landscape.

ATTERTON

Village Earthworks, (Fig 1)   SP353983

The hamlet of Atterton has evidence of shrinkage and changes of use in several areas. These include "Smith's Croft" (2) and an adjacent area (1) at the west end of the village, (surveyed June 6th 1984) where several building platforms could be seen (x). Further evidence of abandoned crofts is visible on aerial photographs in Home Close (3), and immediately to the south on the opposite side of the road (4). Towards the east end of the village a house (6) was cleared away at some time between 1849 and 1885, and a cottage (5) in more recent times. The Tithe Map marks Osier Beds at (7) and (8), and also indicates "Chapel Flat" (9), presumably adjacent to the site of the vanished chapel (ROLLR Ti/15/1 De 76).

Nichols reports "The chapel (in which divine service was formerly performed once a week) is desecrated: the only fragment constitutes now a small part of the wall of a pauper's cottage." (Nichols J, 1811, p1026.) Mentioned as a deserted medieval village by Hoskins (TLAHS, Vol 22, p242,).

BAGWORTH

Village Earthworks, (Fig 2)   SK452080

East of the present village one field of old pasture land reveals earthwork evidence of former enclosures (3), a lane (1) and house platforms (2).

Bagworth Park   SK4508/4509

The park is first mentioned in 1279, when it belonged to the Bishop of Durham. Almost a century later it had passed to Robert Holland, and by 1411 to Matilda Lovell. William Lord Hastings had licence to impark 2000 acres here in 1474. This later park is shown on Saxton's map of 1576 and noted as still in use in 1641 (Cantor L M, 1970-1, p18). Nichols reports that the house was destroyed in the "great Rebellion. In 1769 the ruins were wholly take down and a farm-house built on the site of the old mansion" (Nichols J, 1811, p990).

Bagworth Moats, (Fig 3)   SK 45420865

Robert de Holland was granted licence to crenellate his dwelling place here in 1318, which implies that a substantial house existed at that time. By 1372 the "capital messuage called a castle" had fallen into decay, and the ponds around the mansion were out of use and in need of repair. In the late 15th century Lord Hastings intended to develop this house, together with Ashby and Kirby Muxloe castles, but there is no indication that he did so here before his arrest and execution. (Cantor L M, TLAHS Vol 53, p31). Nichols considered that the "fair and noble house....surrounded by a great moat.." was built by Sir Robert Banaster in 1616 (Nichols J, 1811, p989).

The present farmhouse and garden is still surrounded by a very substantial rectangular moat (1), now drained (site visit, 21st July 1987). The First Edition O.S. map shows an ornamental pond just to the west of the moat (3).

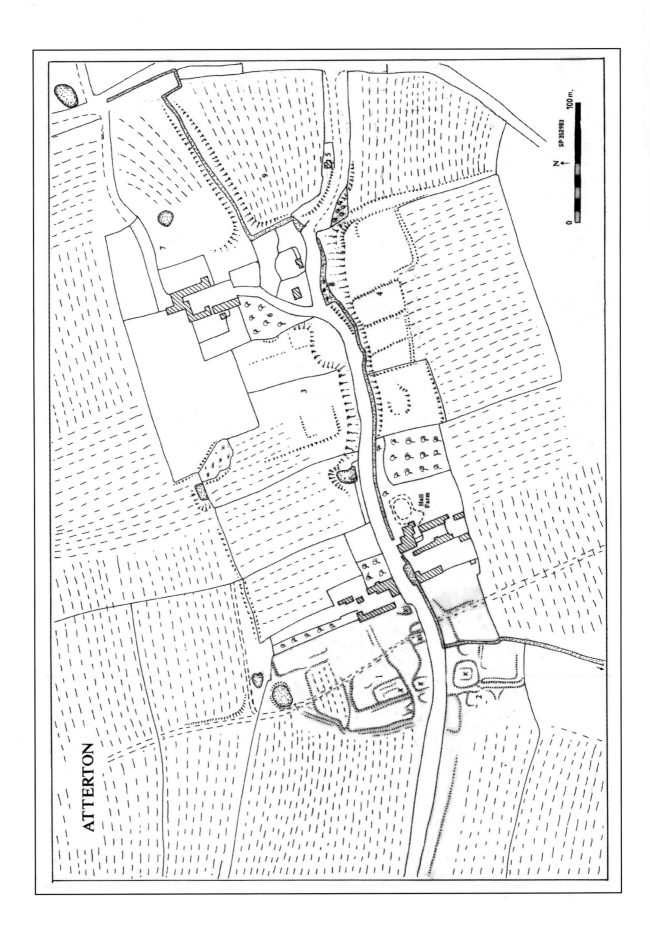

ATTERTON

Fig 1

4

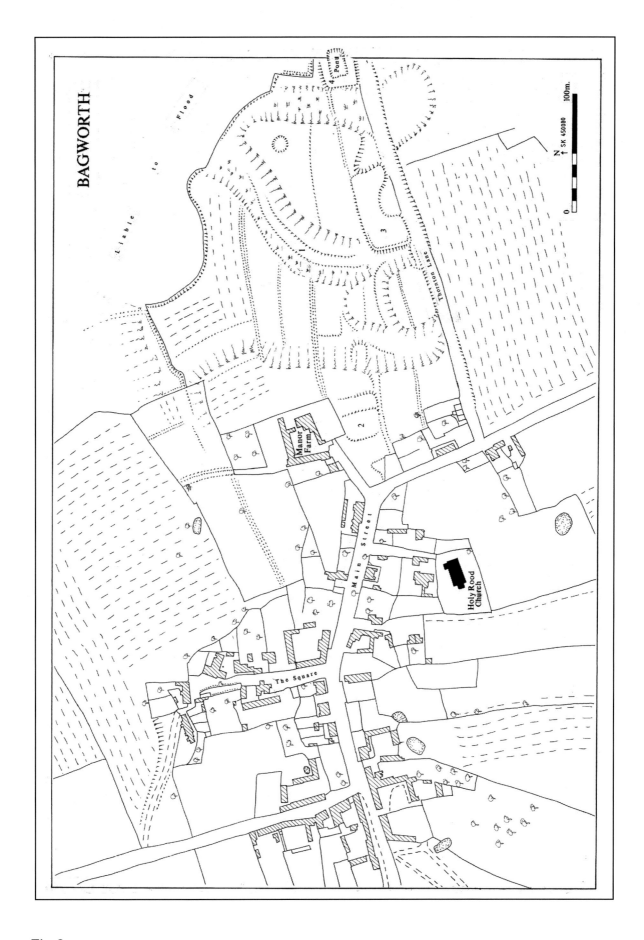

BAGWORTH

Fig 2

5

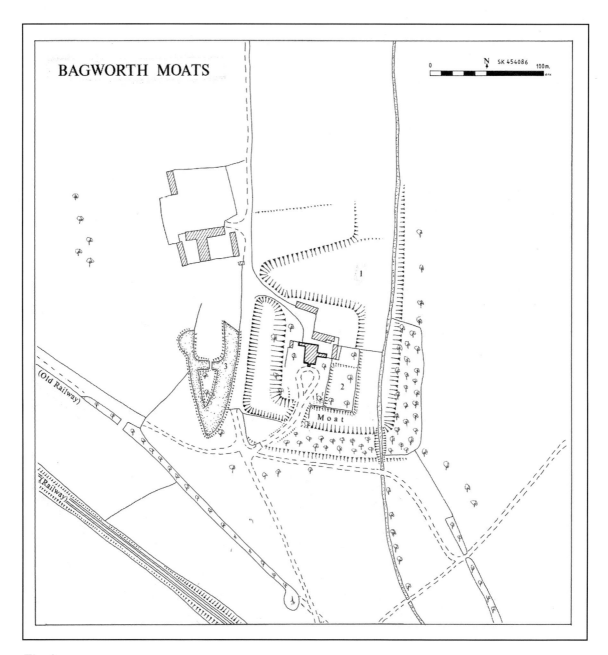

Fig 3

BARLESTONE

Village   *SK 426054*

The open fields of Barlestone seem to have been enclosed at an early date, beginning in 1595 when more than 50 acres of arable land was enclosed by 10 landowners (Hextall, Keith B, 2002, p14). Barlestone was fully enclosed by 1674. During land clearance for a housing estate in 1980 a series of medieval and post-medieval pottery sherds were picked up from the immediate area of the manor house. (Arch Reports, TLAHS, Vol 55, p95)

BARTON IN THE BEANS

Village   *SK395064*

Barton is a village of rectangular plan, with some evidence of changes of plan over the years. There was a chapel, part of the parish of Nailstone, which fell into disrepair and which was succeeded later by a Baptist Chapel.

Fish Pond   *SK401070*
There is an isolated rectangular fishpond to the north-east of the village.

BARWELL

Barwell was enclosed at an early date, between 1625 and 1674, prior to this it seems to have had three fields.

Moated Site, (fig 4)   *SP434957*
Near the site of West Green are remains of a moat. The First Edition O.S. map shows a channel leading from it to a long, narrow fishpond (surveyed 18th Jan. 1989). This is presumably the site referred to by Nichols as follows :- "Captain Shenton's house in Barwell....which is yet in being, and, with a moat about it, is at present a kind of curiosity." (Nichols J, 1811, pp476, note 3)

The site is encircled on its north side by a narrow corridor of land called the Old Drift, which presumably connected the village to West Green. This suggests that the land surrounding the moat might represent an estate taken out of a former area of common.

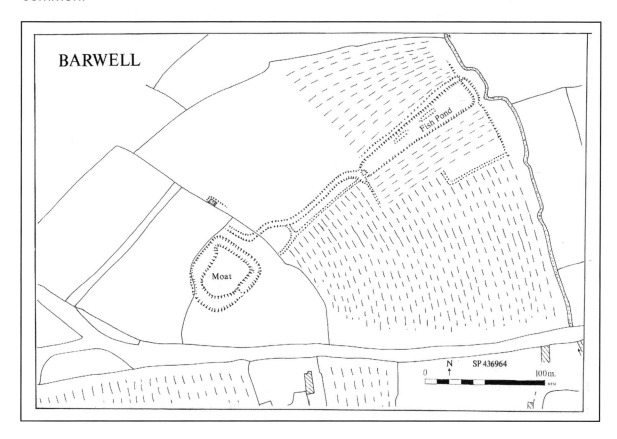

Fig 4

Deer Park, Barwell   *SK435025*
The earliest reference to this is 1209-10 when William Hastings "Owe one palfrey that the Sheriff permit him to enclose his park at Borewell" (Farnham GF, LMVN, p132 quoting Pipe Rolls, 12 John). There is mention in 1312 of a park at Barwell belonging to John Hastings. No further trace of it has been identified. (Cantor L M, TLAHS, Vol 46, p19)

Brockey Farm Moat, (Fig 5)   SP454999

This small isolated moat was levelled in July 1950. At the time it was described as
having inner and outer rectangular moat, the inner one about 30 by 24 yards.
The Ordnance Survey 1:2500 map of 1904 shows a single rectangular moat in a
small enclosure.

The RAF vertical photographs show
traces of a sunken area just east of
the moat - probably a fish pond.
The plan reproduced here
combines information from the
Ordnance Survey and the vertical
photographs. During the levelling
two medieval coffins, lying side by
side, were revealed suggesting that
the site had its own chapel (Arch
Rpts, TLAHS, Vol 28, pp40-1).

Fig 5

BILSTONE

Village Earthworks, Bilstone, (Fig 6)   SK363052

To the east and south of the village an area of earthworks is recorded on RAF
vertical photographs. (RAF 541:212, 3086-8, 8th Dec 1948). These earthworks
consisted of narrow rectangular enclosures behind probable house sites.

"Moat", Bilstone, (Fig 6)   SK362051

On the south side of the village is an "L" shaped pond, which has been considered as
remains of a moat. Inspection on the ground gives no reason to suspect that there
has been a moat here, so it is possible that this feature was constructed as an
ornamental pond. It formed part of the garden of a farmhouse, which is shown on the
1849 Tithe Map (ROLLR Ti/34/1 De76) but had been demolished by the time of the
1904 Ordnance Survey.

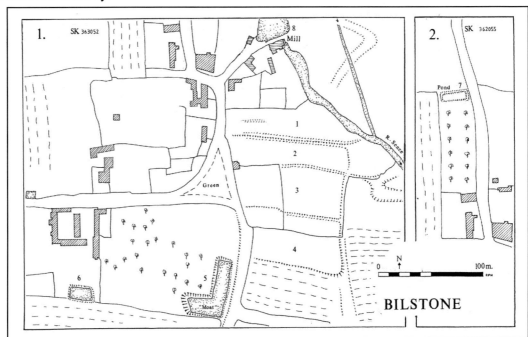

Fig 6

BURBAGE

The Moat House, Burbage, (Burbage 1, Fig 7)   *SP441925*

In the former Rectory Garden is a hollow, identified as a possible moat. This feature appears in an engraved view published by Nichols in 1811 (Nicols J, 1811, pp460+). At that time it was an "L" shaped pond with a circular island at one end, forming part of a formal garden. A bridge spanned the pond with a summerhouse on it. The area enclosed by the pond had geometrical plantings of bushes and shrubs.

The house and garden belonged to one David Wells, who was a Fellow of the Society of Antiquaries. Presumably he kept to the old formal style of garden layout long after it went out of fashion. The Tithe Map of 1841 (ROLLR Ti/54/1 DeXX) appears to show the northern arm of the pond, but nothing else, suggesting that the garden had by then been abandoned.

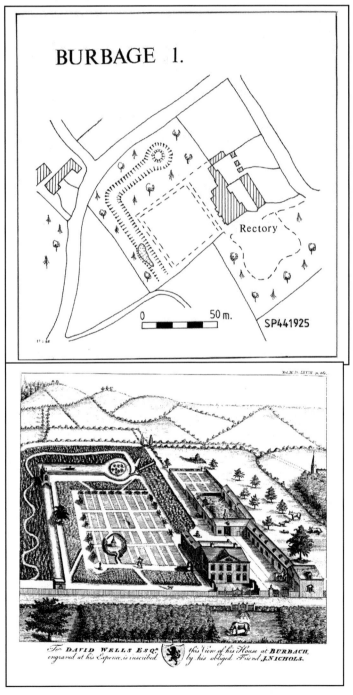

Fig 7

Burbage - Water Mill
SP461903 (Burbage 2, Fig 8)

In the southeast corner of the parish is the site of a medieval water mill. It is remarkable that it was worth building a mill here, on what is only a small stream, just 2.5 km from its source.

Where the stream passes below the Watling Street and enters Leicestershire a man-made channel diverges and follows the valley side for a distance of some 800m to the mill site. At the time of a site visit in spring 1989, there were remains of a substantial stone mill building, beyond which the channel turned through 90 degrees to return the water to the stream. This may be the water mill recorded as being held by Isabel de Hastings in 1325.

Fig 8

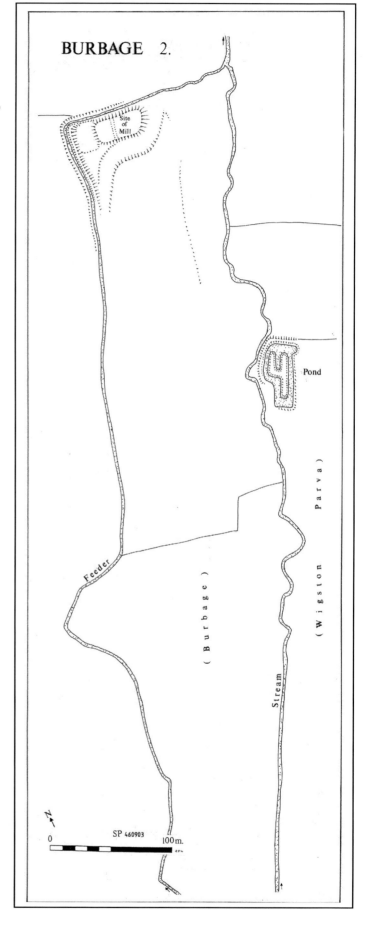

BURBAGE 2.

Site of Mill

Pond

(Burbage)

Stream

(Wigston Parva)

Feeder

N

0   SP 460903   100 m.

10

Burbage Park   *SP4494*

Henry de Hastings held a park here in 1266, and in 1312 Edward Hastings his descendant had two parks, held of the Prior of Coventry. The underwood and herbage were worth 20 shillings yearly.

After this they disappear from the record, and are not mentioned in Inquisitions of 1335 and 1368. (Cantor L M, TLAHS, 1970/1, p20). The park or parks presumably lay in the area of the modern Park House (or Park Farm), near to Burbage Common and Sheepy Wood.

Sketchley, Burbage   *SP423921*

The small village of Sketchley in the parish of Burbage is now surrounded by housing and industrial developments. It was formerly a hamlet of Burbage, and lay in the parish of Aston Flamville. There was once a chapel, but it had gone by 1622. In 1790 there were 8 houses with 27 inhabitants. (Nichols J, 1811, pp468). An evaluation followed by a watching brief was undertaken by ULAS in 1995 in advance of a proposed development at Sketchley Hall. Although a little residual pottery was recovered, no definite archaeological features were uncovered suggesting the focus of the deserted medieval village of Sketchley must lie to the south and south-west of the area investigated. (Arch Rpts, TLAHS, Vol 70, p158).

Smockington, Burbage   *SP455898*

The hamlet of Smockington now in the parish of Aston Flamville lies on the Watling Street. At the time of the Domesday Survey there were ten villeins and six bordars recorded, and there was a mill (Nichols J, 1811, pp469). The village originally lay half in Leicestershire and half in Warwickshire. It was well known to travellers and in the 19th century had a blacksmith and two inns, the Red Lion in the village and the Greyhound at Smockington Hollow (White W, 1846, p536).

CADEBY

Village Earthworks   *SK423023*

Aerial photographs reveal earthwork remains around the Manor House, including a hollow way leading down to the stream, and a small rectangular fish pond. A watching brief in 1999 found no evidence of medieval activity (Arch Rpts, TLAHS, Vol 73, p86).

Naneby Village Earthworks, (Fig 9)   *SK434025*

Naneby is one of the smaller deserted villages of Leicestershire. "The village, which formerly was of considerable note, contains but one house at the present." "The chapel is gone to ruins." (Nichols J, 1811, p522).

The house noted by Nichols is the present Naneby Hall Farm, and it seems likely that most of the visible earthworks have resulted from post-medieval gardens associated with it.

Features recorded on a site visit in 1989 included building platforms (1,2) south west of the farm, and a possible area of post-medieval gardens south east of the farm, including terraces (3,4,5), a fish pond (6) and the sites of two small buildings (7,8). The earthworks were surveyed in the spring of 1987.

Nichols records some documentary references to the village, beginning with the Itinerary of 1280. In the Lay Subsidy of 1445 Naneby was rated at 10s 6d, but with an abatement of 1s. (Nichols J, 1811, pp522).

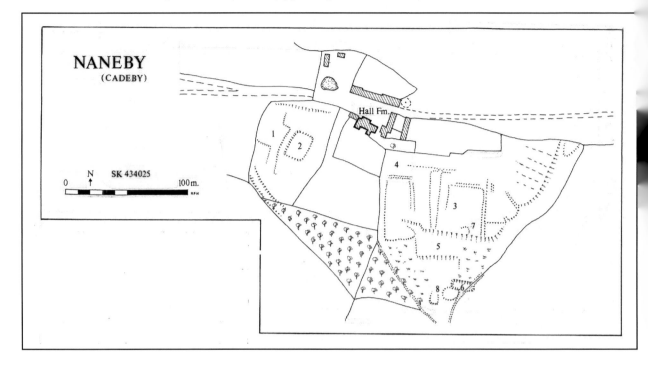

Fig 9

Deer Park, Cadeby   *SK435025*
Evidence in the form of field names suggests the former existence of a deer park in this area, northeast of the village. There were three parks in the medieval manor of Market Bosworth. One was north of the village and a much larger one was to the south that could be this one.

CARLTON

Village   *SK394049*
Carlton is a small village of irregular plan near to Market Bosworth. The First Edition Ordnance Survey maps show a number of small ponds in the village. There may be a mill site here.

CONGERSTONE

Village Earthworks, (Fig 10)   *SK366054*
North-west of the parish church are earthwork remains including three house platforms (1,2,3) and parts of three levelled terraces (4,5,6) below which is a rectangular area (7) once enclosed by banks and ditches on its north and south sides and a fishpond (8) on the west side. It seems likely that this enclosure formed part of the gardens of a vanished manor house located north of the church (9) but this is as yet speculation. These would appear to be part of the curtilage of a vanished manor house site. (Air photos RAF 541:212, 3086, 8th Dec 1948).

Glebe terriers of 1625 record the names of three open fields, Middle Field, Moor Field and Lynch Field.

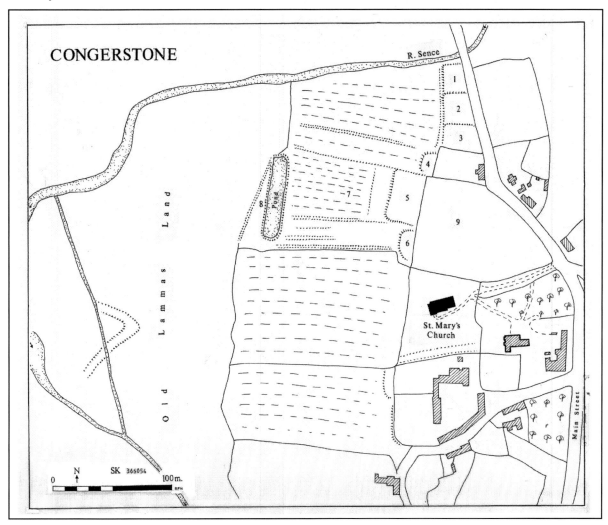

Fig 10

DADLINGTON

Village   *SP404980*
The banks and hollows in the centre of the village have been interpreted as moats, but seem mostly to have been created by gravel quarrying. Nichols reports "Dadlington Green – from whence gravel is fetched to repair the highways." (Nichols J, 1811, p714) There are several ponds and some minor banks and ditches.

Dadlington Moat   *SP39679818*
The Victoria County History mentions a moat at this site but nothing is now visible, nor is it marked on the Ordnance Survey map of 1888.

DESFORD

Water Mill, Desford   *SK485042*
Desford water mill is on the Heathe Brook and was supplied with water by a leet 500m long.

Fish Ponds, Desford, (Fig 11)   SK490034

Near Bullockhall Barn, alongside the stream, are the earthwork remains of three long narrow fishponds (1,2,3), surveyed on May 4th 1987. In addition there are two very small ponds (4,5) likely to be stew ponds or breeding tanks.

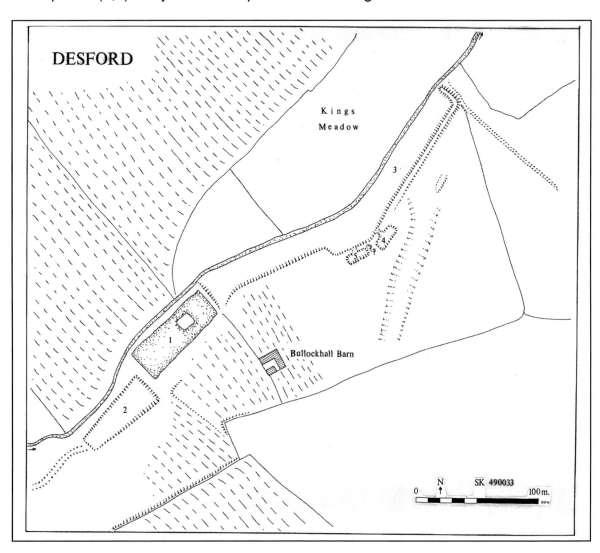

Fig 11

Barn Park, Desford   SK50035

The Park was probably created by one of the Earls of Leicester during the 12th century on the western fringes of Leicester Forest. It is mentioned in 1297 and in 1419 when it was part of the Duchy of Lancaster estates. It certainly existed in the 1530s when Leland visited it. At that time the Keeper of Barn Park was one of the forest officers managing the area for the Crown. It inclosed and area of approx 250 acres(Fox & Russell, 1948, p26). According to Burton it was still in use in 1641. (Cantor L M, TLAHS, Vol 46, p18). However by the early 17th century it had long since fallen into disuse (ibid, p20). There was still a distinct estate of Barrons Park which appears on 19th century maps (ROLLR 3D42/Mii/1 "Survey of Barrons Park Estate of the late J.E.Carter Esq, 1813", Ti/89/2 De76, "Barrons Park", 1849, and Dg19/Ma/89/1 "Plan of the Township of Barrons Park", 1849). Park House appears on the 1834 OS map.

Lindridge Moat, Desford, (Fig 12)   SK472046

An isolated rectangular moat (1) survives near Lindridge House Farm, and may either represent the site of an isolated medieval manor house or, more probably, the remains of a medieval or later moated garden for which an 18th century (?) sketch plan is in the Record Office (ROLLR reference unknown). The surrounding field has been levelled by ploughing in recent years, but old aerial photographs show a pond (2) and additional enclosures (3,4) around the moat.

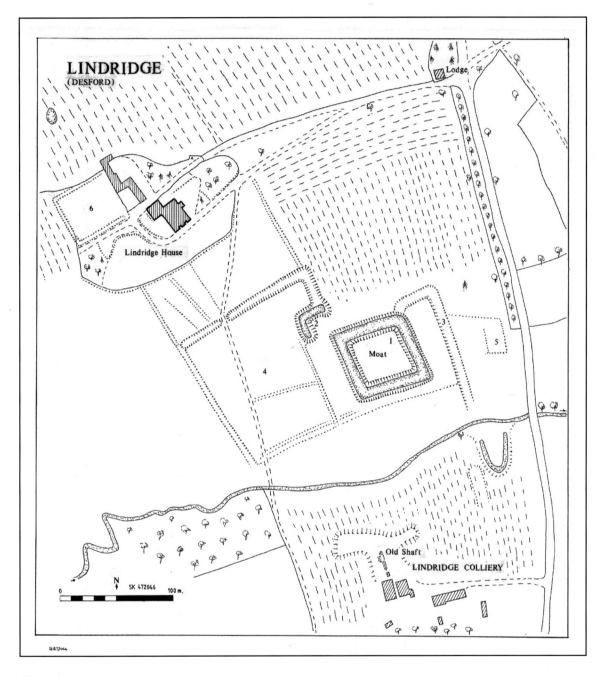

Fig 12

EARL SHILTON

Castle, (Fig 13)   *SP47059821*

The castle mound, surrounded by a ditch, lies just west of the parish church, in a field once known as "Castle Yard". The castle was probably built by the Earls of Leicester in the 12th century and served to guard the western approach to their hunting chase of Leicester Forest. It may have had only a relatively short period of use. In the 1950s it was adapted as a public park, and a miniature gateway was built with a "drawbridge" across the moat. There are flower beds on the slopes of the mound and a lawn on top. The site was surveyed on February 21st 1982. The church may lie in the castle bailey and may originally have been the castle chapel. Creighton (TLAHS, Vol 71, p31) says that "the castle may have embraced the extant parish church within its defences, as such making a statement of conquest to the existing community."

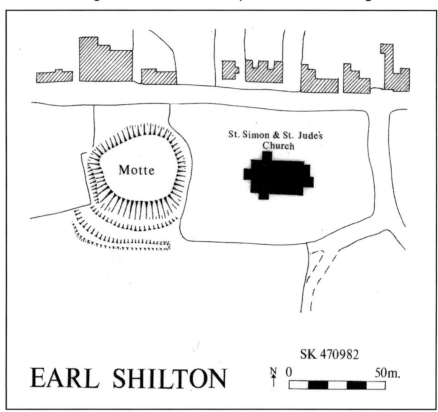

Fig 13

EARL SHILTON

St. Simon & St. Jude's Church

Motte

SK 470982

N   0   50m.

Fish Pond, Earl Shilton   *SP458968*

To the south of Earl Shilton the parish takes in part of a former fishpond. This is one of a series of earthworks in the parish of Elmesthorpe which appear to be the remains of a grand 17th century formal garden scheme associated with the now-vanished Elmesthorpe Hall. There is a plan in Hartley R F, 1989 "The Medieval Earthworks of Central Leicestershire" p62, Fig 52, Leicestershire Museums Arts & Records Publications.

FENNY DRAYTON

Fish Ponds and Village Earthworks, (Fig 14)   *SP390971*

To the west of St. Michael's Church are remains of several fishponds, presumably associated with a vanished manorial site. Aerial photographs show traces of old enclosures to the south, but most of these features have been built over in recent years. The plan is based on a site visit, drawn up in the summer of 1984.

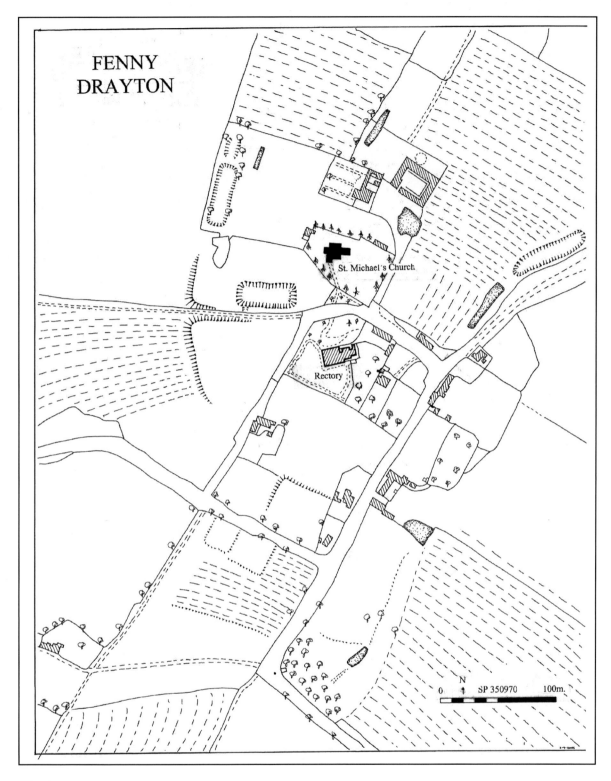

Fig 14

Mound, Fenny Drayton   *SP355973*
This isolated conical mound alongside the Roman Road to Leicester has been
identified as a possible burial mound, but could be a post-Medieval landscape
feature. There is another isolated mound some distance to the south in Higham on
the Hill parish.

GOPSALL

Village and Hall, (Figs 15,16)   *SK352064*

The site of Gopsall village has not been located, but it seems likely that it lay in the area where the post-medieval Gopsall Hall was created although the village was probably long gone by then. A large house with extensive formal gardens replaced the 16th-17th century mansion house in about 1750. This became derelict after the Second World War and was completely demolished. There are surviving garden walls and some garden earthworks, but no positive evidence for the site of the village. (Tithe Map, ROLLR, Ti/125/1 De76, 1850)

Fishponds, (Fig 16)   *SK360064*

The large pond at this location lies across the line of a great avenue of trees running east from Gopsall Hall to the entrance gate at Shackerstone. It is identified as "Fish Pond" on the 1st edition OS map and was probably created as part of the mid-18th century landscape gardens. 300m to the north is the "Duckpond", while 500m to the SW was the site of another large ornamental pond, shown in 18th century views of the Hall.

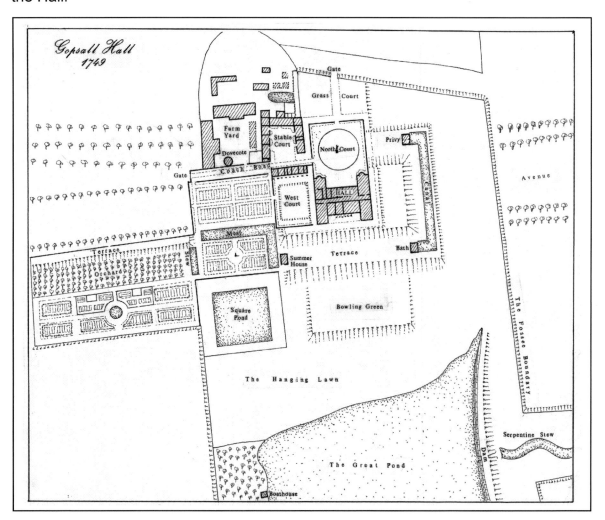

Fig 15, Top of Plan is north

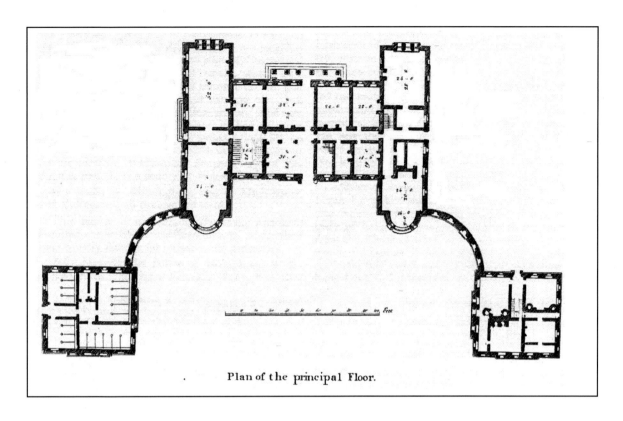

Plan of the principal Floor.

Gopsall – Plan taken from Nichols 1811. Top of plan is south.

GOPSAL HALL.
The Seat of the Rt Honble Sophia Charlotte Baroness Howe,
1811.

Gopsall Hall – View of south front taken from Nicholls, J 1811. Note the side 'wings' and compare to plan of 1749 and later plan of 1885 (next page).

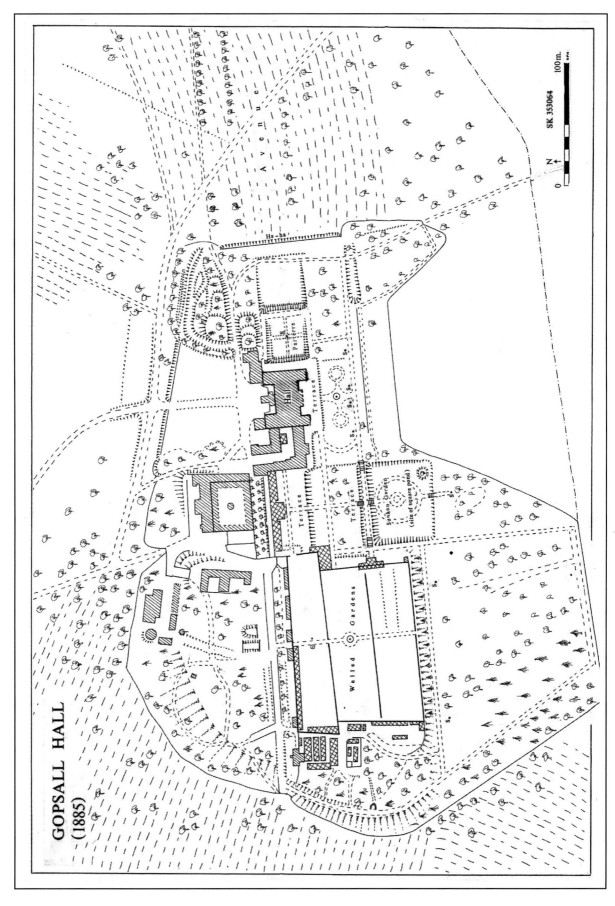

GOPSALL HALL (1885)

Fig 16

GROBY

Groby Castle, (Fig 17)   *SK 5239 0764*

The Old Hall and Castle Hill at Groby used to be a dramatic and picturesque sight. Now the embankment of the Groby by-pass overshadows them and much of their context has been destroyed. Castle Hill (1) is a kidney-shaped mound, up to 7 metres in height, which used to be surrounded on its north and east sides by a semi-circular section of bank (2) flanked by inner and outer ditches. The survey was carried out on Spring 1984. Further to the north, before construction of the by-pass, there lay an area of rectilinear enclosures (3), sloping downwards to two rectangular fishponds (4,5) and a stream. This was presumably an area of gardens and orchards associated with the Old Hall. Excavation on the castle motte before the construction of the bypass showed that it had been deliberately slighted (presumably in 1176) and was built around a pre-existing stone tower. Perhaps an Anglo-Saxon church tower or part of a thegn's fortified residence. For a discussion of the excavations in 1962/63 see Creighton O, TLAHS, Vol 71, pp22-25.

The castle is said to have been built by the Earl of Leicester during the third quarter of the 12th century, and destroyed by the forces of Henry II in 1176 (Cantor L M, 1977-78, p36). Later the site became the seat of a branch of the Ferrers family, and passed to the Greys by marriage in the mid 15th century.

Sir Thomas Grey, 1st Marquess of Dorset, began to enlarge the buildings, and put up a brick gatehouse, but then, in about 1500, decided to build on a completely new site in his deer park at Bradgate instead.

Leland, quoted in Nichols, notes the fact that the mount became part of a garden, as follows : "...the ditch of the Motte was filled up by Sir Thomas Grey....entending to make an herbare there..."

Burton, quoted in Nichols, writing in about 1600, says that "The castle was utterly ruinated and gone and only the mounts, rampires and trenches were to be seen." (Nichols J, 1811, p631)

Fig 17

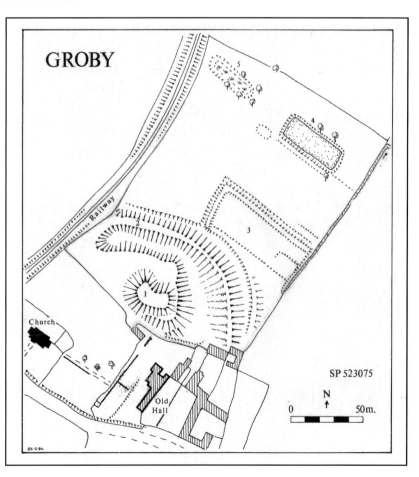

VIEW OF GROBY, S.E.

Vol. IV. Pt. CIV. p. 634.

N.E. VIEW.

Park, Groby   SK5008

The Park of Groby is first mentioned in 1288, held by William de Ferrers. In 1325 it was described as being divided into two parts, and in 1445 it contained "beasts" - presumably cattle. A palisade is mentioned in 1512, and Leland noted in 1540 that the park had a circumference of six miles. (Cantor L M, 1970-1, p21)

The park included the present Martinshaw Wood ("The Shaw"). Also within the park was a fishpond called "le Over Pole", perhaps commemorated by a field name "Fish Pond Meadow" at SK 505082. There was also a warren, presumably indicated by "Coneygree Yard". The area had been disparked by the mid-17th century. The curving boundaries are evident on the Markfield Tithe Map of 1849 (Ti/216/1) and later large-scale O.S. maps.

Lady Hay Wood, Groby
(Fig 18) SK517084

A rectangular earthwork feature was discovered and surveyed by S Woodward and the Groby Archaeological Society in 1984. The considered it likely to have been a ditched enclosure which originally surrounded an isolated medieval lodge or farmstead. However, documentary confirmation of this was lacking (from a note in LCC HER)

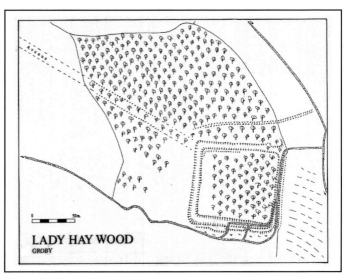

LADY HAY WOOD
GROBY

Fig 18

Fishpond, Groby, (Fig 19)   SK530076

The dam of this pond is still evident.. On the map of 1757 (ROLLR PP443/1-2, "Map of the Manor of Grooby", by John Doharty, 1757) the area is marked as "Pool-tail Meadows" and the pond was presumably out of use. There is reference to a fishpond in 1512, but this could equally refer to Groby Pool.

Groby Pool and Water Mills   SK520082

The first mention of Groby Pool is probably in 1147, when an inquisition taken after the death of William de Ferrers refers to two pools and two water mills. Writing in 1540, Leland noted that Groby pool had been supplying fish to Leicester Abbey, and that the stream from the pool drove a mill. A study of the sediments by Carol David of Loughborough University suggested that the pool was possibly created in the 12th century A.D. (Ramsey D, 1995, pp30-33).

David Ramsey's article also points out that the site of the Medieval mill is marked on Doharty's map on the north side of Groby Pool (SK52140843) and was supplied with water by a leet (traces of which survive) from the vicinity of Old Wood. This mill was replaced in about 1820 by one constructed at the outlet from Groby Pool (SK52350825) There are still remains of a 19th century sawmill at this location, but the area has been disturbed by quarry development and is heavily overgrown.

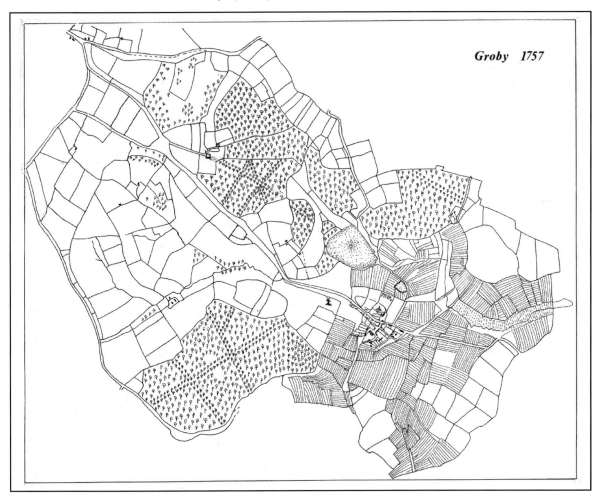

Groby 1757

Fig 19

HIGHAM ON THE HILL

Village Earthworks, (Fig 20)   SP384954
North of St. Peter's church is an area of earthworks indicating former village closes along an old lane, drawn up following a site visit on April 19th 1989. There are house platforms (1,2,3) north west of the church. An adjacent area north of the church (9) contains another house platform (4), sites of several small ponds (5,6,7,8) and another platform representing the site of one or more buildings (10). Nearby is an old lane (11) and a large fish pond in the Rectory grounds. Both of these appear on the map of 1807 (ROLLR QS47/2/9 "Map of the Parish of Higham, including Lindley and Rowden", 1807). The plan was drawn up after a site visit Spring 1989.

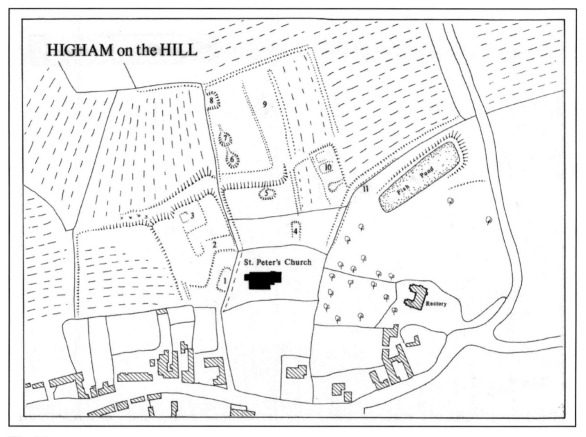

Fig 20

Lindley Village, Moat and Hall, (Fig 21) SP365958
Nichols reports that Lindley "In the Conqueror's Survey this lordship is called Lilinge". It is recorded as having nine villeins and three bordars with three ploughs. (Nichols J, 1811, pp645) The village gave way to a 16th century mansion house, depicted on the frontispiece to Burton's history of Leicestershire in 1622. At that time the house, with its stable yard, orchards and ornamental flower garden, lay surrounded by a rectangular moat. Nearby was the medieval chapel, illustrated as a substantial ruin used for agricultural purposes by Nichols in 1793.

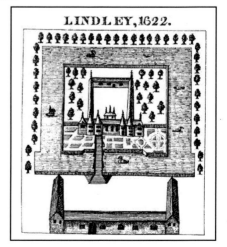

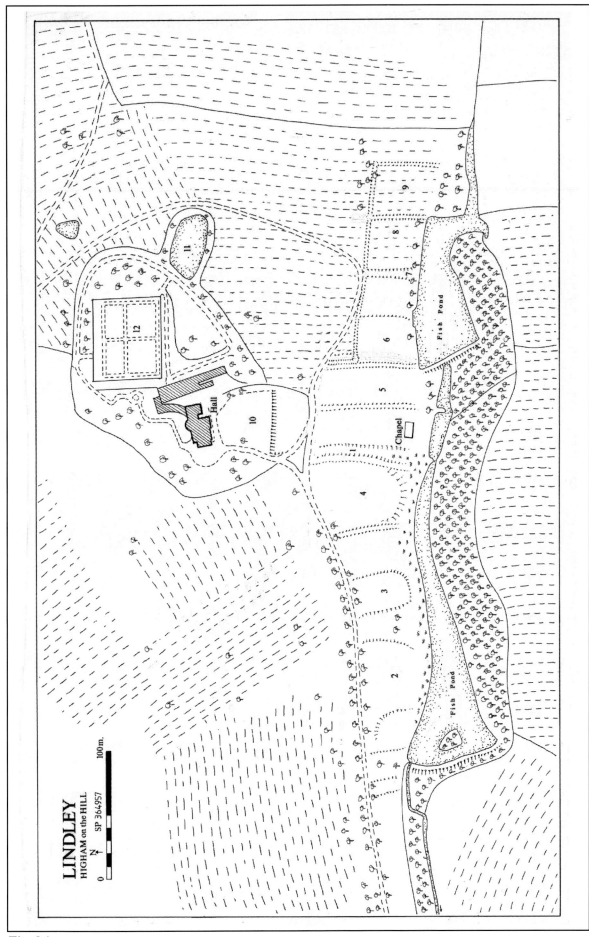

LINDLEY
HIGHAM on the HILL
SP 364.957

Fig 21

A new Lindley Hall (10,11,12) was built to the north of the moated site on the hilltop in 1705, and the moat was partly filled in at that time, and completely eradicated in 1774 when the area was modified into two long ornamental ponds.

LINDLEY CHAPEL, 1793.

Some earthwork evidence remains around the site of the chapel (1-9), and fragments of medieval pottery have been observed in the adjacent ploughed field. (Medieval. Settlement Research Group Annual Report Vol 10, 1995, pp31-2)

An aerial photograph taken by James Pickering shows soil marks north of Lindley Hall indicating a former rectangular enclosed area and a circular mound (perhaps an ornamental mound) surrounded by a ditch. Much of the area of Lindley was levelled for the construction of Nuneaton Airfield in the 1940s, but its appearance is recorded on a detailed map of 1807 (ROLLR QS47/2/9).

Lindley Park   SP365970
A map of 1808 shows four field names, Hither Park, Little Park, Middle Park and Further Park at this location, adjacent to Lindley Wood.(ROLLR, Ma/141/1 "Map of Lindley and Rowden in the parish of Higham", J Eagle, 1808).

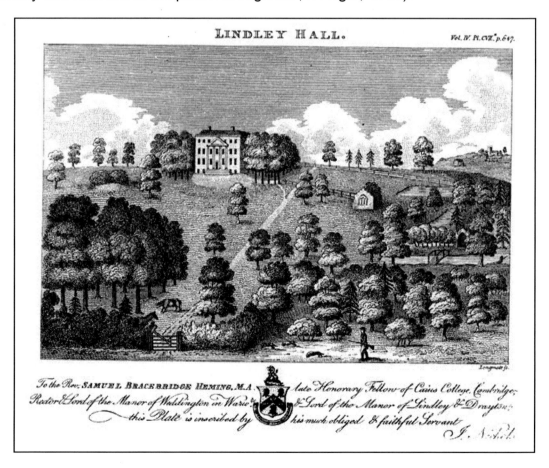

LINDLEY HALL.

Rowden   *SP366964*

Nichols reports Rowden as "a distinct manor…consisting of one large farm house and about 300 acres of land; and it lies so near Lindley Hall, that part of the land is comprised in the Lawn" (Nichols J, 1811, p647). A map of 1808 (ROLLR Ma/141/1) identifies Rowden as a separate estate, perhaps an area of old woodland, which had by then been cleared. Rowden House Farm survives, but most of the estate was cleared to make way for a wartime airfield in the 1940s.

HINCKLEY

Hinckley Castle, (Fig 22)   *SP428938*

Substantial earthworks survive to the north of Hinckley Parish Church. The castle was founded by the Earls of Leicester and was probably in existence by the middle of the 12th century. By 1361 it seems to have been abandoned, and is referred to as "a plot called the castle" (TLAHS, Vol 53, P34). Nichols records that "the antient site of the Castle had, beyond the memory of the oldest inhabitant, been occupied as a gardener's ground, and the Castle-hill considerably lowered by taking materials for repairing the roads; till, in 1770 Mr. Hurst caused a handsome modern dwelling house to be built." (Nichols J, 1811, p677).

Creighton comments, "the earthworks are often misquoted as a ringwork. In fact the surviving earthworks represent a substantial bailey, the motte having been entirely obliterated by development. Its surrounding ditch was recorded during construction work in 1976". (TLAHS, Vol 71, p34)

The Castle House was demolished in the 20th century, and the top of the mound adapted as War Memorial gardens. Part of the ditch encircling it has been dammed to form a duckpond.

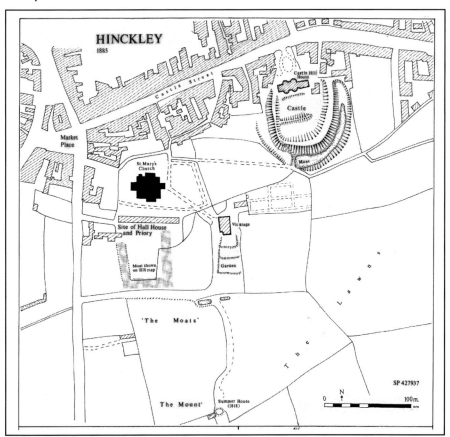

Fig 22

Immediately south-east of the parish church was the site of the Hall House or Priory. Nichols has a view of this building as it looked c.1800. (Nichols J, 1811, p680+) The Plan of the Town of Hinckley, made in 1782, shows three sides of a moat enclosing the Hall House on its south side, with another pond a little way to the east. An early 19th century map of the parish shows two more ponds lying to the south-west (ROLLR Ma/142/2, De1225/246, Map of Hinckley, 1818). It may be significant that at this time the site of the Hall House, moat and ponds all belonged to the Dean and Chapter of Westminster.

Nichols identified the site as being formerly the Benedictine Priory. The whole area has since been built over and no trace can be seen. The Priory was an alien cell. Recent small scale excavation by Hinckley Fieldwork Group has uncovered walls of this complex.

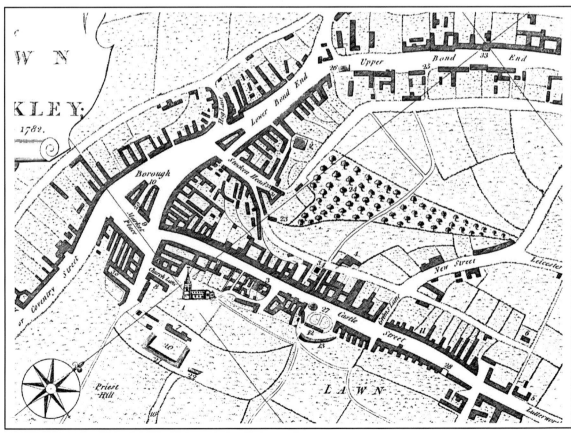

Hinckley Deer Park   SP4393

The area of the medieval deer park has been largely built over in the 20th century. Nichols estimated its location as follows: "The original situation of the park is easily to be traced. *The Lawns* still so called, which were a beautiful pleasure ground, divided it from the Castle of Hinckley, its northern boundary; on the South it extended to Burbach; on the East to the East Wood, the Stocking and the Outwoods; and on the West to the borders of the parish." (Nichols J, 1811, p454 note 1).

The park was in existence in 1297, when it was called "Scydleye Park" and belonged to the Earls of Lancaster (successors to the Earls of Leicester). In 1323 there is reference to the sale of "herbage" from the park and to the cost of fencing part of the pale. By 1507 it had passed to the Crown estates and George Hastings held the office of Keeper. By 1588 it was being leased out and probably ceased to be a park shortly afterwards. (Cantor L M, TLHAS, Vol 46, p21)

Wykin Village and Garden Earthworks, (Fig 23)   SP409952

To the south of Wykin Hall there was formerly a fish pond (1) and an "L" shaped section of ditch (2) enclosing part of the gardens. On the east side of the orchard was another pond (4) while the Tithe Map (see below) indicates a further one (3) later covered by the farmyard and buildings. The ditch was noted by Marcus Paul Dare and tentatively identified as a moat, but there is no evidence for the other two sides ever having existed.

To the west (around 5) there used to be earthwork remains of four rectangular enclosures, which appear to have been an area of the medieval village. The site was levelled at some date before 1979 and no trace is now visible. This area is named as "Hall Close" on the Tithe Map of 1845 (ROLLR Ti/142/2, Wykin Tithe Map. 14th March 1845, John Thorpe).

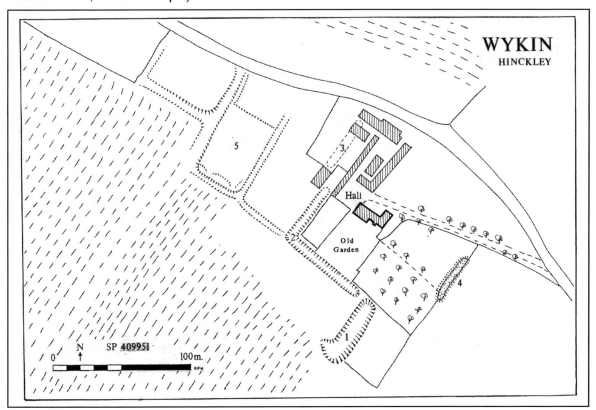

Fig 23

The Hyde   *SP396920*

This triangular area of land, although lying to the south of the Watling Street, was part of Leicestershire until the late 19th century. Nichols has a reference to a chapel here at the time of King Edward III. Quoting a Dr Thomas he notes further "there is only one house standing here, near which are yet to be seen the vestigia of this depopulated village." (Nichols J, 1811, p722).

KIRKBY MALLORY

Village Earthworks, (Fig 24)   *SK455004*

Around All Saints Church and the rectory are earthwork remains of what was presumably part of the village, with a rectilinear pattern of enclosures and house sites.

There are foundations of two buildings (1,2) and what appear to be older house platforms (3,4,5,6,7). West of the church is the ditch of an old enclosure (8) with others recorded on aerial photographs to the east (9,10). Between the church and the hall is a small pillow mound, perhaps a rabbit warren or a parkland feature such as a pet's grave.

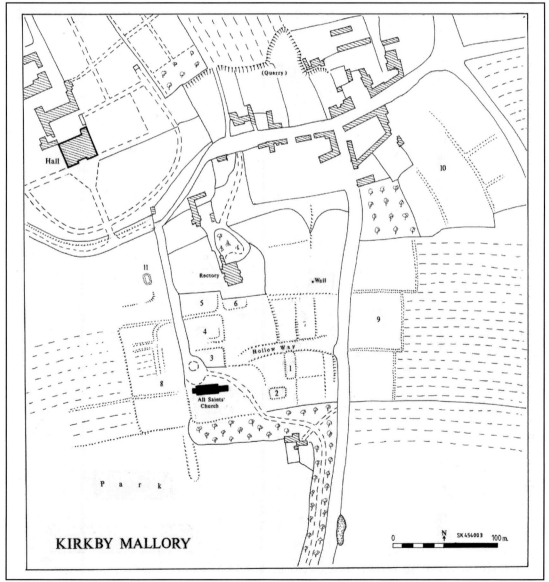

Fig 24

Kirkby Hall, (Fig 24) — SK452005

An amenity park was laid out south and west of the hall, probably in the 16th century. Amongst the features of the parkland were three fishponds (SK450005) from which water channel led to the site of a small water mill. A plan dated 1755 (ROLLR, reference unavailable) shows the park extending to Kirkby Wood and including a complex series of ponds and channels, the water mill and a windmill. The plan and drawing below are from Nichols.

The Hall was requisitioned by the military during World War II and demolished in 1953. The subsequent development of the Mallory Park racing circuit has greatly changed the appearance of the area. During work to create fishing ponds several elm water pipes were uncovered, suggesting that the system of water supply to the gardens was even more elaborate than shown on the 1755 map.

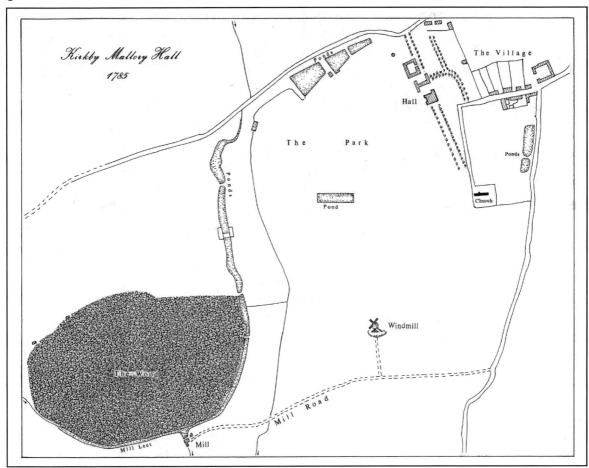

Kirkby Moats, (Fig 25)   SK454018

The O.S. 1st Edition 1:2500 map of 1885 shows this as a large and complex moated site with three concentric moats, one outside the other. It was used as a rubbish tip in the 1970s and largely filled in by 1980, so it is difficult now to say much about its original function. There is a possibility it could be a 15th Century garden feature. It was located in an isolated part of the parish and might perhaps have been a park lodge.

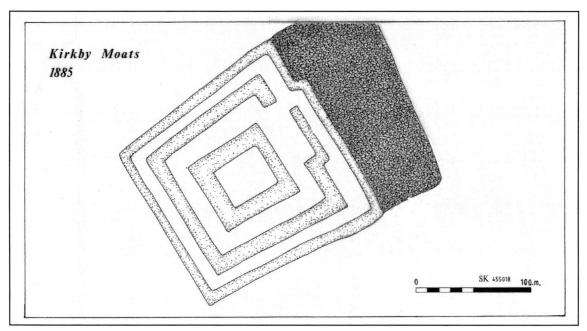

Fig 25

MARKET BOSWORTH

Bosworth Hall, (Figs 26, 27)   SK408033

The Hall was at the height of its importance in the early 18th century, and formal gardens were created around it. These included a parterre (1) on the south side of the Hall, with moats (2) on two sides, and a forecourt (3) on the west side, extending into a paddock (4) flanked by fruit trees. These features are shown on a survey made in the 1820s (Plan of a Mansion House etc, belonging to Sir Willoughby Wolstan Dixie, Bart.).

The O.S 1st Edition 1:2500 map of 1885 shows a sunken garden (5) immediately east of the Hall, and an avenue of trees (6) extending east from the moat, flanked by a walled garden (7) and "The Wilderness" (8) and leading to an Ice House (9).

To the north of the Hall are further earthwork features, including fish ponds (10-14), an area of old garden terraces (15), enclosures (16,17), and two mounds (18,19) - probably "prospect mounds" or tree mounds. Prospect mounds enabled owners and their guests to obtain a view of the garden so as to appreciate its layout and symmetry.

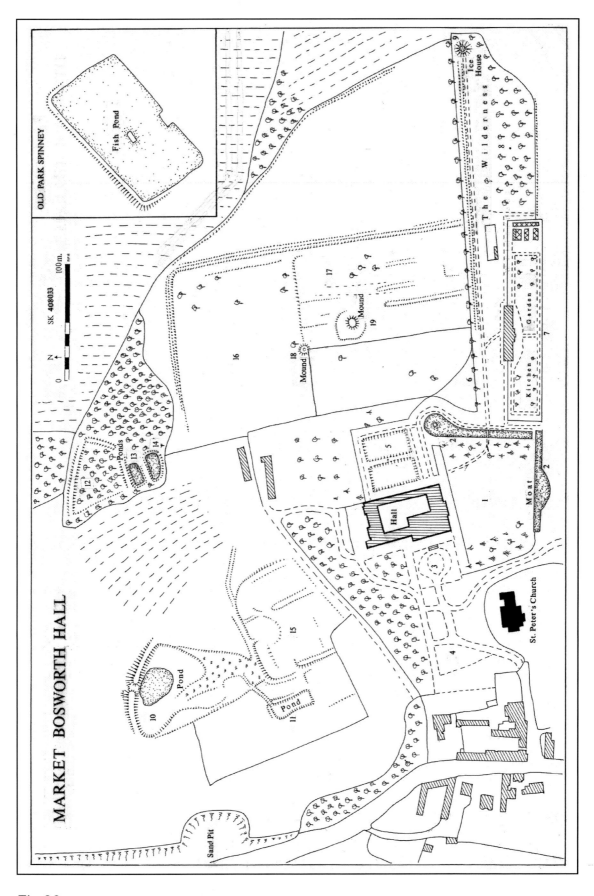

Fig 26

33

Deer Park (Southwood Park)   *SK4102*

The curving boundaries of this park are still apparent to the south of Market Bosworth, enclosing an area of woods and grassland, and including several fishponds. They show well on the Cadeby Tithe Map of 1841 (ROLLR Ti/61/1 DE 76). The park is mentioned in 1232 and 1293. (Cantor L M, TLAHS, Vol 46, p22)

An 18th century plan shows "the wood within Bosworth Park" dissected by a geometrical pattern of rides, and containing features such as the Looking Glass Pond and the statue of Hercules (which still survives).

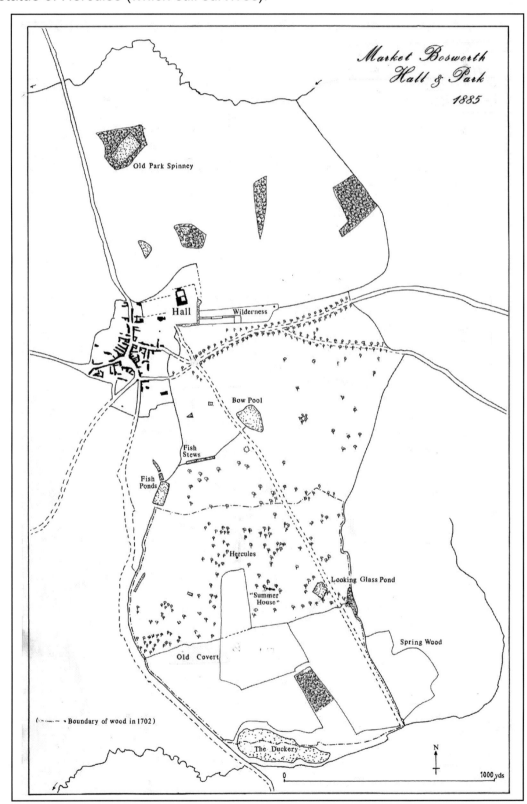

Fig 27

Deer Park (Old Park)   SK407035
Several "Old Park" field names north of Bosworth Hall indicate the area of this deer park, which is mentioned in 1232, when Robert de Harcourt held it, and again in 1293. There are earthwork remains of several fishponds (five noted above under Bosworth Hall), and another large pond by Old Park Spinney, as well as sections of bank and ditch (Cantor L M, TLAHS, Vol 46, p22).

Water Mill   SK401043
This water-driven corn mill with its millpond lay a mile or so to the north of the town. It is mentioned in 1294 (Foss P, 1993, p12).

Coton Village Earthworks, (fig 28)   SK387020
Coton is a hamlet with at least two settlement nucleii. The majority of the evidence is at Far Coton, with earthworks defining a clear area of settlement. There is a hollow way (1) flanked by sites of buildings (2,3,4,5) behind which are old enclosures (6,7,8). Nichols relates that there was a chapel here, dedicated to St Anne, and that the remains of this building were dug up in 1700 on the north side of the hill. There are slight traces of old settlement in the form of earthworks near Coton Priory Farm.

MARKFIELD

Markfield Village   SK4910
The village of Markfield grew up on the edge of the open waste of Charnwood, and originally comprised several separate arable fields with open common and trackways dividing them. Glebe terriers of 1630 record three open fields, Nether, Middle and Over. There are references to the pasturing of cattle and pigs on the commons, the putting up of temporary buildings to house them, and to the gathering of dry wood for fuel. (Nichols J, 1811, p797.)

Markfield Fish Ponds   SK487097
Two long narrow fishponds are marked on the Tithe Map of 1849 (ROLLR Ti/216/1) at this point. They probably formed part of the gardens of a medieval manor house.

Groby Park (Markfield)   SK496092
Much of the area of the medieval deer park of Groby lies in the parish of Markfield, around Little Park Farm. The curving line of the park pale shows on large scale O.S. maps and on the Tithe Map of 1849 (ROLLR Ti/216/1)

WINDMILL on MARKFIELD HILL, 1792.

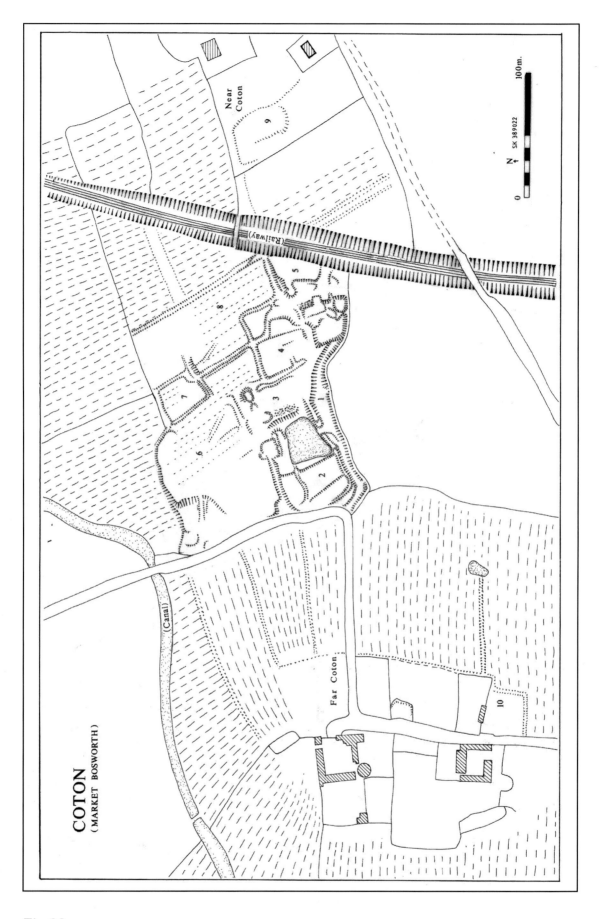

COTON
(MARKET BOSWORTH)

(Canal)

(Railway)

Near Coton

Far Coton

SK 389022

N

100 m.

0

Fig 28

36

NAILSTONE

Village Earthworks and Ponds, (Fig 29)   *SK418072*

RAF vertical air photos (RAF 541:212) show earthwork evidence both north and south of the church, indicating the former extent of the village. Those on the north side have been built over again in recent years. The First Edition O.S. 1:2500 map shows two long narrow fish ponds, one south-east of the church at SK419070 (below the Manor House) and one north of the village at SK416074. A windmill ("molendinum ventriticum") is mentioned in 1279 (Nichols J, 1811 p807)

Deer Park, Nailstone Wiggs   *SK426086*

A park belonging to Henry de Hastings is mentioned here in 1266, but nothing more is known of it. (Cantor L M, TLAHS, Vol 46, p23). Nailstone Wiggs was a wooded, boggy area in the north-east corner of the parish, which was perhaps the wood "three furlongs long and two broad" mentioned in the Domesday Book. It was destroyed by tipping from Nailstone Pit in the late 19th/early 20th Century.

Fig 29

37

NEWBOLD VERDON

Hall and Formal Gardens, (Figs 30, 31)   *SK441038*

The present Hall was built at the end of the 17th century, and a large formal garden was created to the south of it.

The Hall (1) is approached from the east by an entrance courtyard (2) which still has traces of its original geometrical patterned cobbling. The courtyard had a pavilion at each corner, and three of them survive, adapted as farm buildings (3,4,5). North of the Hall are walls remaining from the former kitchen gardens? (6) To the south of the Hall is a rectangular garden (7), enclosed on three sides by a moat. This is flanked on its west side by a winter garden probably created originally as a "wilderness" garden with another moated area (8) and two small ponds (9). Returning to the main axis of the gardens, which runs southwest from the Hall, there is an overgrown plantation with remains of a small pond (10) and a boundary ditch including another pond (11). From this point there are earthwork remains of an avenue which bisects a circular sunken garden area (12) with two more probable ponds (a,b).

Flanking the avenue on one side is an area dissected by linear ditches (13) and a bank (14). This area also probably represents an area of former gardens and plantations. Beyond them are two long, narrow fish ponds (15,16).

To the south at SK438030 are remains of a larger fishpond, and there were two even larger ones further south at SK438027 and SK436021. The last two used to have dams crossing the valley, and were partly in Cadeby parish.

Deer Park

A park belonging to Elizabeth de Burgo is mentioned in 1360 (Cantor LM, TLAHS, Vol 46, p23).

Brascote Village, (Fig 32)   *SK443036*

This little settlement is mentioned as having 3 taxpayers in 1327, and 4 in 1332. It is alternately named "Brocardescote". (Nichols J, 1811, p824)

The village disappears from the records after 1445, but the name remains and at the time of a site visit, c1990, there was earthwork evidence for the site of the village just north of Manor Farm. There are several probable house sites (1,2,3,4) set in old enclosures and a fishpond (5) nearby. Across the lane is another enclosure (6) and the foundations of a substantial building (7).

NORTON JUXTA TWYCROSS

Manor House Moat   *SK324068*

A moat is recorded existing just to the west of the Manor House. The site has been built over in recent years and there is now no trace of a moat. Across the road, to the west, was a long narrow fishpond marked on OS 1:2500 maps, now filled in. The village had four open fields in 1679; Stoneford, Leasowe, Church and Mill.

Moat or Pond   *SK322071*

Immediately west of the churchyard is an "L" shaped pond, possibly the remains of a small moat. .

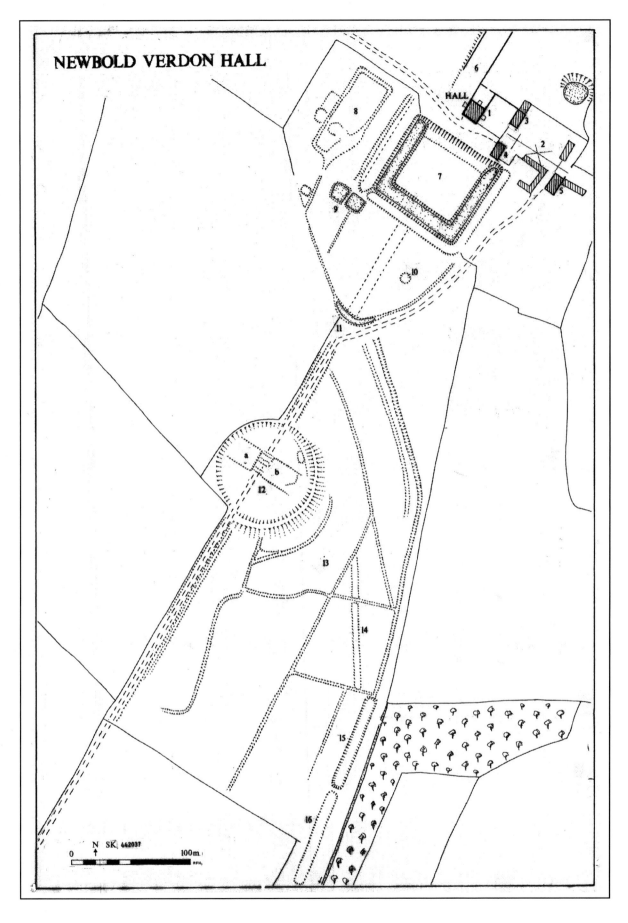

NEWBOLD VERDON HALL

Fig 30

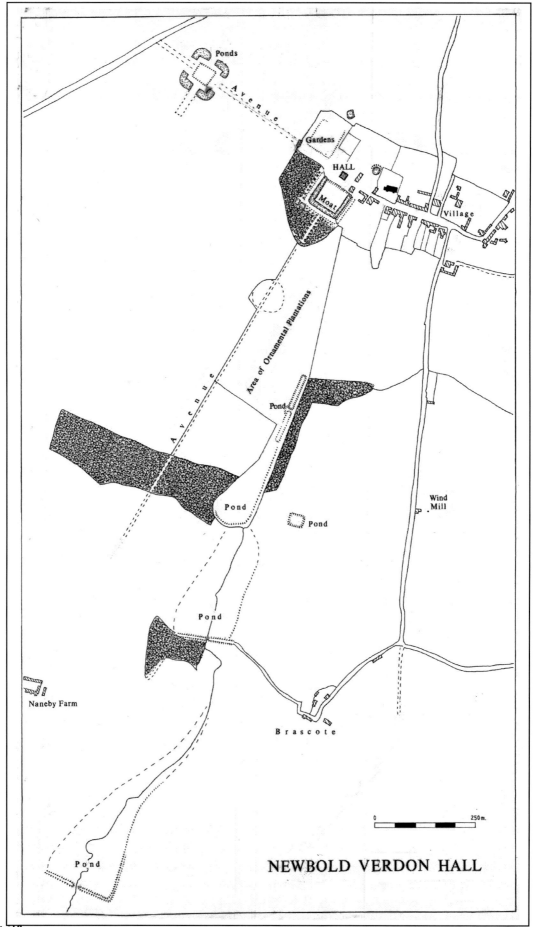

Ponds

Avenue

Gardens

HALL

Moat

Village

Area of Ornamental Plantations

Avenue

Pond

Pond

Pond

Wind Mill

Pond

Pond

Naneby Farm

Brascote

0   250 m.

NEWBOLD VERDON HALL

Fig 31

40

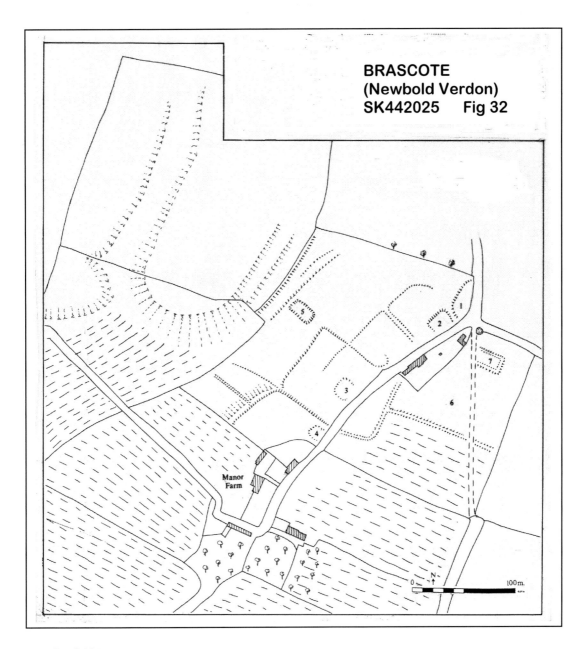

Manor
Farm

100 m.

ODSTONE

Village Earthworks, (Fig 33)   SK392078
The village of Odstone has remains of a small area of abandoned settlement south-east of the Hall. The plan was drawn up after a site visit in December 1989. Aerial photographs indicated a former area of village (1) showing as soil marks, with possible house sites (x). There was a pond further down the hillside (2). Landscaping around the Hall prior to 1900 included additional ponds (3,4) in an area of old orchard, and a round pond just west of the Hall.

South-east of the Hall is a terraced garden, probably dating from the 19th century, and further south is a raised terrace (7) marking the site of a demolished building or garden feature.

Help-Out Mill   SK379078
This was one of the last working watermills in Leicestershire. It is now a private house and part is used as a restaurant.

41

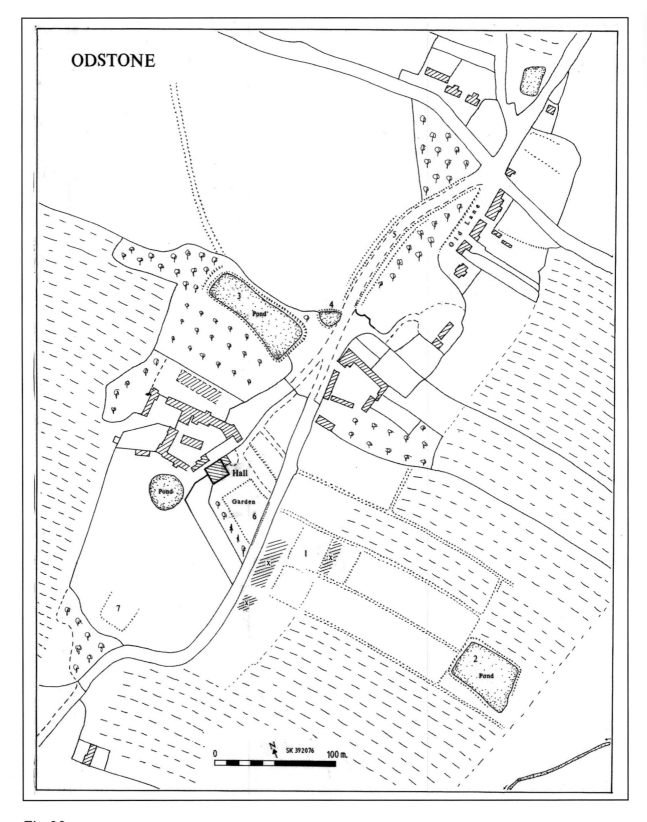

ODSTONE

Fig 33

42

ORTON ON THE HILL

Village Earthworks, (Fig 34)   *SK306038*

RAF vertical air photos (RAF 541/212 3094-6, 8th Dec 1948) reveal extensive evidence in the form of earthworks surrounding the present village. In particular, one area of the village (1) seems to have been cleared to allow the creation of Orton Park, and in the southern corner of the village earthwork platforms represent the remains of substantial groups of buildings (2,3). The village may formerly have extended further to the southwest as well (4).

Lea Grange, (Fig 35)   *SK322055*

Around the present Lea Grange Farm are earthwork remains of the medieval grange farm, including traces of enclosures. There are rectangular building platforms (1,2,3,6) and two level areas (4,5) partly enclosed by moats. (plan next page)

The entire site is enclosed by two by-pass channels (7,8) dug to take water from the stream around the grange site. This feature is common to several grange farms in west Leicestershire. At the lowest point of the site are two fishponds, one with a triangular island.

The estate belonged in the medieval period to Merevale Abbey, part of the gift of the Abbey's founder, Robert de Ferrariis.

A plan of the estate of Lea Grange (illustrated right) was published by John Nichols (Nichols J, Vol 1, Part II, P53 in "Additions and Corrections in Vol IV".

Nichols also quotes a sale description of the estate in 1815. It "comprises an antient messuage, several cottages, and extensive farm buildings, and nearly 320 acres of land". The estate was sold in three lots with each field numbered and names (see Nichols J, Vol 1, Part 2, p152)

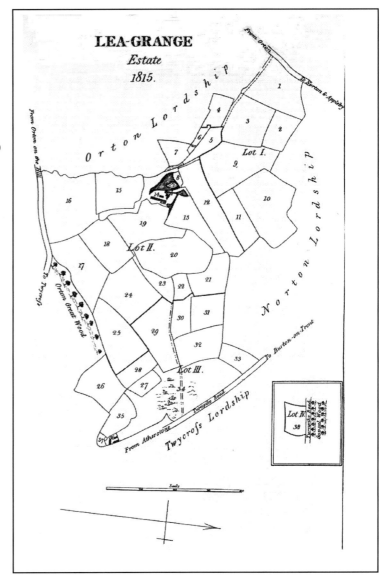

Plan of the estate for the sale, Nichols Vol 1 Part 2, Plate 53, p151

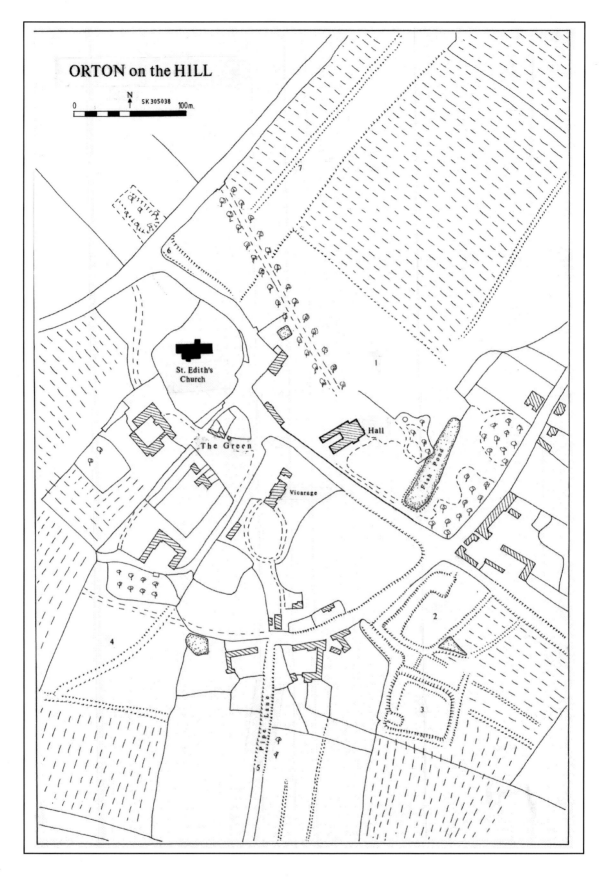

ORTON on the HILL

0   SK 305038   100m.

St. Edith's
Church

The Green

Hall

Flash Pond

Vicarage

Pipe Lane

1

2

3

4

5

6

7

Fig 34

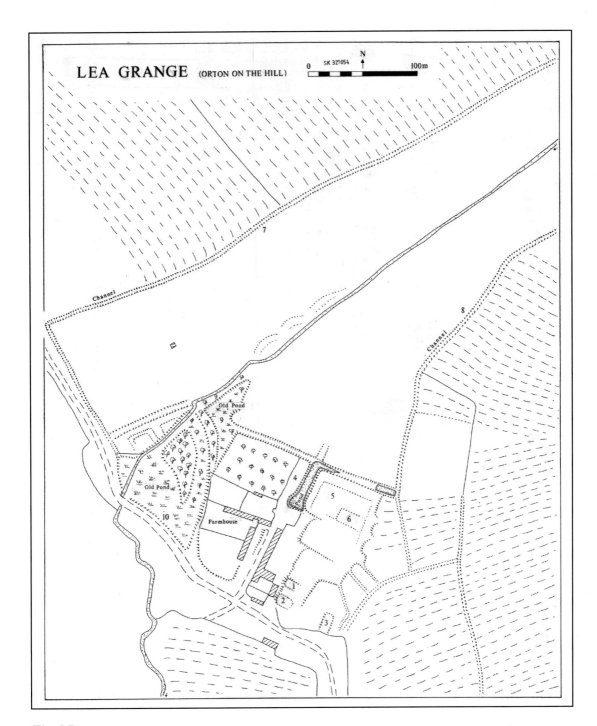

Fig 35

OSBASTON

Osbaston Hall, Park and Village   *SK424044*

Osbaston Hall and its gardens have been superimposed onto the plan of this small village. There are some slight village earthworks, but more conspicuous are the fish ponds associated with the Hall, which appear to be part of a 16th or 17th century garden scheme. Three fields north and east of the Hall have "Park" names on the 1850 Tithe Map, indicating an area of probably post-Medieval amenity park bounded on the west by the Hinckley to Ibstock road, and on the north by the stream on the parish boundary.

Osbaston Windmill Mound(s)   SK419050

This large mound, covered with trees, lies in Mill Field and presumably marks the site of the village windmill. Another mound has been identified on aerial photographs, at SK423041 and could also be a windmill mound.

PECKLETON

Village Earthworks, Moat and Fishponds, (Fig 36)   SK468008

Peckleton village lies on the course of the Roman Road from Leicester to Mancetter, which forms a prominent hollow way through the village. There are some old enclosures and a probable house site (1) north-west of the church. The Manor House has remains of a rectangular moat (2), to the north of which there was formerly a mill (3) and millpond (4), marked on old maps. West of the Manor House is a hollow way (5) flanked by traces of former buildings (6,7,8). Further west, at SK464009 are remnants of a dam (9) which formerly retained a large fishpond, called the Pool Tail on old maps. North of the village, at SK470013 are two surviving ponds in a field called Fish Pond Close.

Tooley Park   SP4799

The park of Earl Shilton, or Tooley Park, was part of the estates of the Earldom of Leicester in 1279. It passed to the Duchy of Lancaster and so to the Crown, and in 1507 George Hastings held the office of Keeper as a sinecure. It is shown on Saxton's map, and described by Burton as being still in use in 1641. The park occupied a large area between the Leicester to Earl Shilton road and the village of Peckleton. Remnants of the park pale can be seen for several hundred yards along the north verge of the road. Tooley Hall was built in the park in the post-Medieval period and much of the deer park remained in use as an amenity park until the end of the 19th century. The estate is mapped out in detail on the Tithe Map of 1852 (ROLLR Ti/252/1), which records a number of "Park" field names.

Fishponds

Two fishponds are marked on the Tithe Map of 1852

RATBY

(including and see also GROBY)

Burgh Park   SK496062

This park may originally have been created within the existing earthwork ramparts of Bury Camp, which is considered to be a late Iron Age hill fort. The park seems to have originated in the early 13th century, perhaps under the ownership of Saer de Quincy, and then probably been enlarged for Roger de Quincy (1219-1264) or Anthony Beck (c.1284-1310). It is mentioned as part of the property in the Manor of Whitwick in 1270. The park seems to have been based on Old Hays, and in its later years filled the area between the open fields of Ratby on the east, and the enclosures of Old Hays and Bondman Hays on the west. The estate and house of Old Hays were granted to Leicester Abbey in about 1310, but there is no further mention of the park and it may have become defunct at this time or shortly after.

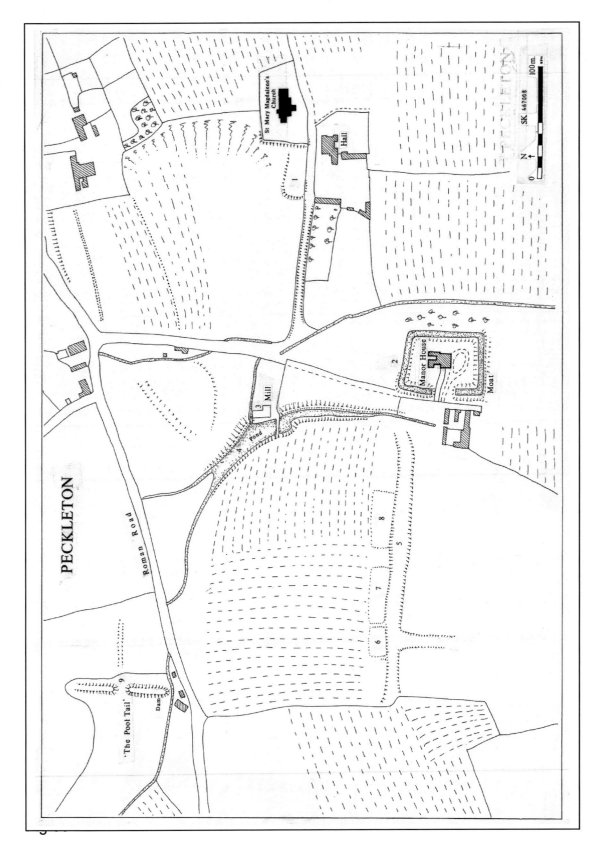

Old Hays, (Fig 37)   *SK490064*

The farmhouse of Old Hays (1) is surrounded by a rectangular moat, crossed by a decorative stone bridge (2). Although its present appearance is largely post-Medieval, its origins go back into the twelfth or thirteenth centuries, when it was created as a defensible manor house in an assart enclosed from the Waste of Charnwood. North of the moat are two levelled terraces (3,5) defined by banks and ditches, and probably representing areas of former garden and orchard. Between them is the site of a small building (4).

Ratby - Newtown Unthank
SK491043
The name of this hamlet suggests that it was created as a new settlement in the parish of Ratby in late Medieval or early post-Medieval times.

Ratby – Whittington
SK486083
The name Whittington (surviving in Whittington Grange and Whittington Rough) suggests the possible former existence of a village, but there is no archaeological evidence to support this theory.

Fig 37

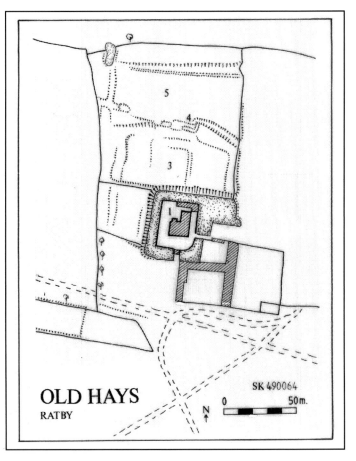

OLD HAYS
RATBY

SK 490064

0   50m.

RATCLIFFE CULEY

Village Earthworks, (Fig 38)   SP327994
Earthwork features both north and south of the village show how the plan of the settlement has changed. To the east of the church is a low circular mound (1) surrounded by a ditch or moat. This was been identified as a castle, but would seem to offer little in military terms as a defensive site. It could have been the site of a timber-framed manor house, and it is surrounded by other features including a fish pond (2).

South of All Saints' Church is the Hall Field with an old fishpond - the Lady Pit - on its west side (3). Close by are traces of a small building (5) and another pond (4). A small platform (6) just north of the church, indicates the site of an old cottage. There is evidence of another area of former village some 250 metres north of the church.

SHACKERSTONE

Village Earthworks and Mound, (Fig 39)   SK375069
125 metres north-east of St. Peter's Church is a mound (sometimes referred to as "The Mount") which has been interpreted as the site of a castle (1). Old maps of the village reveal that a mansion house stood between the church and the mound in the 18th century (2). It seems likely that the mound was then part of a scheme of landscaped gardens created around this house. It might have had a summer house on top, offering views over the gardens and the surrounding pastures.

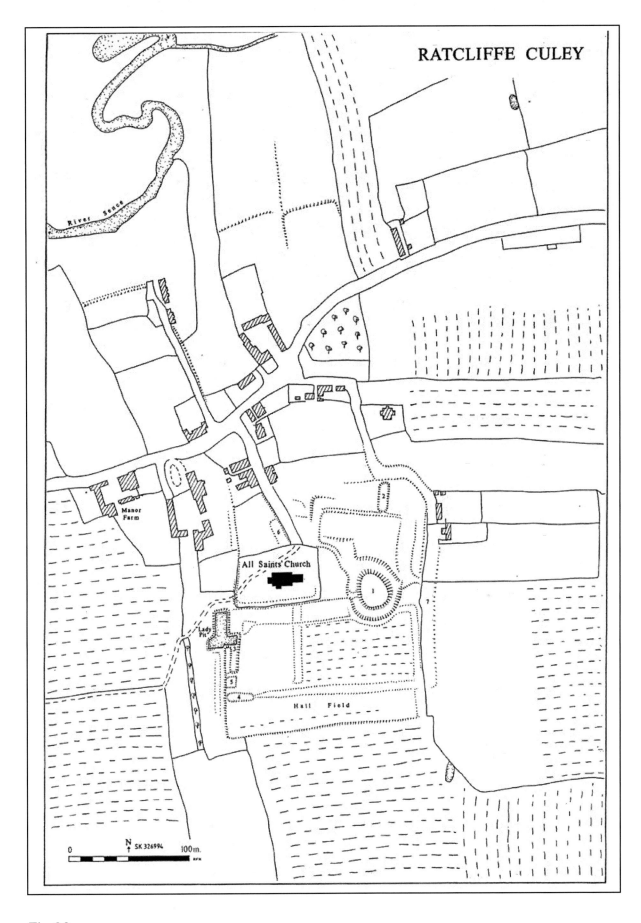

RATCLIFFE CULEY

River Sence

Manor Farm

All Saints Church

Lady Pit

Hall Field

N
SK 326994
0   100m.

Fig 38

49

A trench dug in 1940 located remains of a possible central post, about 14" in diameter, and a rectangular chamber (note by F Cottrill in Leicestershire County Council Historic Building Sites & Momuments Record). There are other earthwork features around the village, including level platforms (3,4), a pond (5), and the sites of two buildings (6,7). Further south, near Arnold's Farm, was a small moated site (8) and other features including a levelled platform (9) and a hollowed-out area (10) which has been interpreted as a possible fishpond. These features were surveyed by the late Arthur Hurst, and details are in the Leics HBSMR.

Shackerstone had four open fields in 1679; Congerstone Field, Hill Field, Far Field and Catto Field.

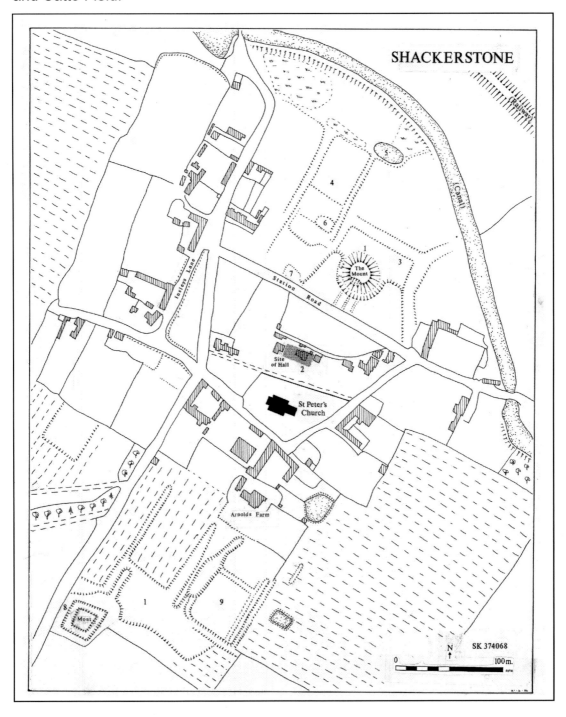

Fig 39

50

SHEEPY MAGNA

Village Earthworks and Fish Pond, (Fig 42)   SK325010
Glebe terriers of 1679 record three open fields; Little Field, Middle Field, and Little Sheepybrook Field.

Earthwork remains indicate the former extent of the village at its south end, between the road and the River Sence (1,2). An additional area south of All Saints Church was probably levelled in the 18th or 19th century to create gardens (3) around Sheepy Hall. A number of changes in the village plan can be observed by comparing modern maps with a plan dating from 1820 (ROLLR En/Ma/286/1 De248 A Map of Great Sheepey by J Eagle)

Ornamental Ponds   SK326016
South of the village is a curious shaped arrangement of fishponds. It might be expected that these would be related to a scheme of parkland or gardens and a mansion house, but there is no indication of this. (Shown on En/Ma/286/1)

New House Grange (Fig 40)   SK318024
This was a grange farm of Merevale Abbey and formerly had several earthwork features.

There was an "L" shaped moat (1) enclosing the south end of Dove House Yard with the dovecote (6), while to the east of the tithe barn (5) was an orchard with a narrow moat (2) on three sides. There were also two small ponds (3,4) near the barn.

These features appeared on the 1903 Ordnance Survey maps, but have since been filled in.

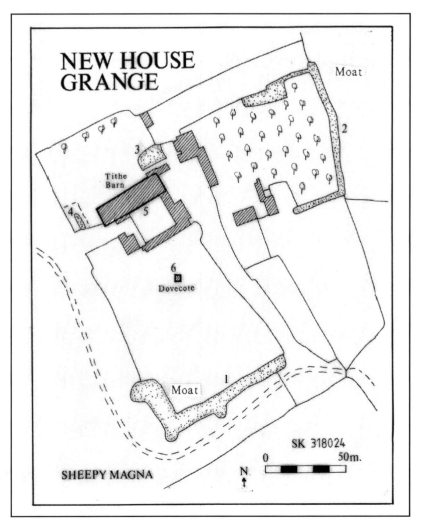

Fig 40

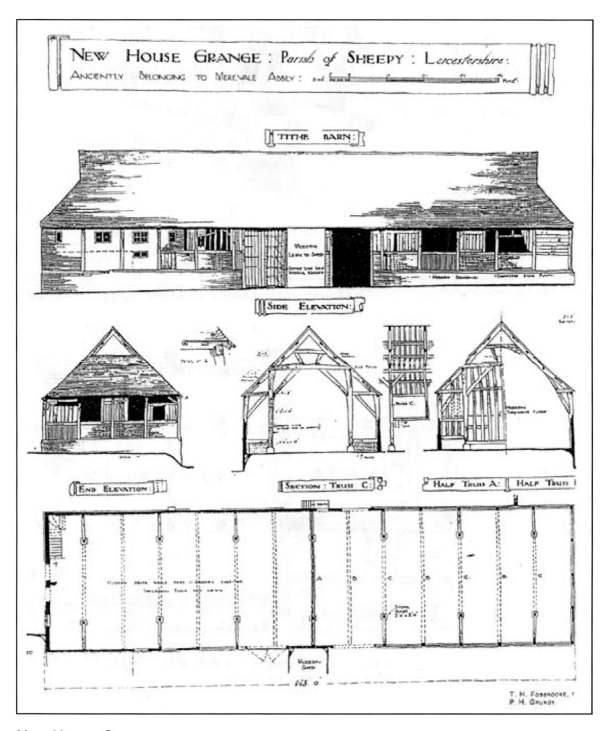

New House Grange

The Mythe   SK315995

The Matriculus of 1220 makes reference to a chapel here, and in 1279 Sewall
Tuchey possessed a capital messuage with a water mill and fishing rights. There is a
further mention of the messuage in 1349. The Liberty of Mythe, comprising 200
acres, was purchased in 1615 by Thomas Baylie, Citizen and Vintner of London.
(Nichols J, 1811, p938.)
The First Edition Ordnance Survey map of 1885 shows The Mythe Farm with a long
narrow pond to the north of it which has been interpreted as a possible moat,
although there is no definite evidence of this.

Pinwall Grange, (Fig 41)   SK304006

Some distance north of Pinwall Grange Farm, on the far side of the Tamworth to
Atherstone road, is an isolated moated site representing the site of the medieval
Pinwall Grange. Within the remains of a rectangular moat are traces of foundations
of a small circular building (1), perhaps a dovecote. The hollow nearby may be the
robbed-out foundations of the farm house.
To the south the moat extends into a possible fish pond (3), while to the east is an
enclosure (4) defined by banks. There are traces of two more small ponds (5,6) and
the old course of the stream (7). As at Lea Grange, the stream has been diverted into
two channels (8,9) which enclose the whole of the grange site.
Pinwall belonged in the 15th century to Merevale Abbey, and was surrendered by
them in 1539. It was subsequently granted in 1541 to Sir Walter Devereux as part of
the Abbey's estates.

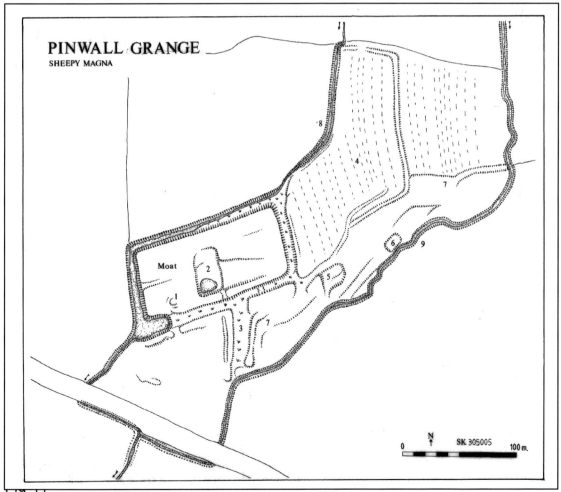

PINWALL GRANGE
SHEEPY MAGNA

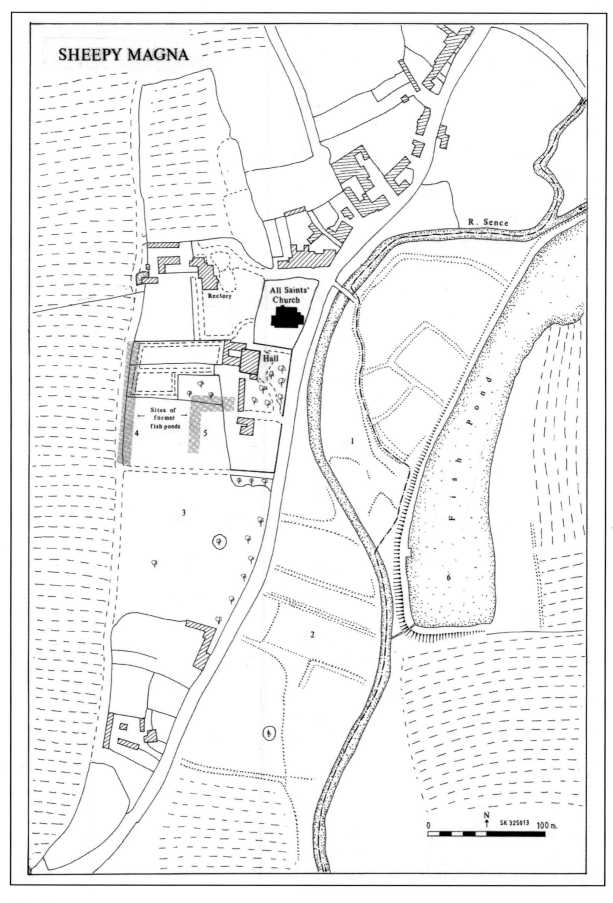

SHEEPY MAGNA

Rectory

All Saints' Church

Hall

Sites of former fish ponds

R. Sence

Fish Pond

1

2

3

4

5

6

N

SK 325013

0   100 m.

Fig 42

Moorbarns, (Fig 43)   SK300032

This was the site of the deserted village of Weston, described as having had five ploughlands, lying waste during the reign of King Edward the Confessor, but worth 70 shillings at the time of the Domesday Survey in 1086. There was a chapel here, and the place was excused from the tax of Peter Pence in 1344. It was granted in the reign of Henry II by Robert de Ferrariis to Merevale Abbey and subsequently enclosed as a grange farm.

The estate of 308 acres, within a ring fence, was purchased by the Steeles from the Bradshaws around 1640. The site had been abandoned by the 19th century, and the earthworks were levelled by ploughing in about 1960 but the plan can be reconstructed from RAF vertical photos taken in 1948 (RAF 541:212 4046-7, 8th Dec. 1948). These show several areas (A,B,C,D,E) enclosed by substantial banks. These probably represent the livestock enclosures on the grange farm. Near the centre of the site are a number of probable building platforms (f,g,h,j,k,l,m). The first five of these could represent either parts of the medieval village or the grange farm. The last two sites (l,m) are large and apparently isolated structures which could well be buildings from the grange.

As at other grange sites, the original stream course has been abandoned, with the water instead led along ditches which enclose the site. There was a pond in the centre of the site and one near the northern corner. A little to the east was another hollow (n), originally either a quarry or a pond.

Glebe terriers of 1679 record three open fields in Sheepy Magna; Little Field, Middle Field, and Little Sheepybrook Field.

SHEEPY PARVA

Village Earthworks and Mill, (Fig 44)   SK332013

There is earthwork evidence of the former extent of the village to the south (1,2), north (3)and east (4) of the existing houses. The course of the River Sence has been altered by the creation of a pond and channels for Sheepy Water Mill, and a large fish pond.

SHENTON

Village and Garden Earthworks   SK385002

There are slight traces of village earthworks around Shenton, especially to the north-west of St. John's Church. Shenton Hall was developed from the 16th century onwards and the creation of its park and gardens, particularly the series of long ornamental ponds, has remodelled the south and east sides of the village.
Some additional detail of changes in the village plan can be gleaned by studying the map of 1727 (6D43/31)

SIBSON

Village, (Fig 45)   SK354009

The village was finally enclosed in 1803. Prior to this there were three open fields, named in 1679 as Mill Field, West Field (Towards Sheepy), and Towards Bosworth Field.

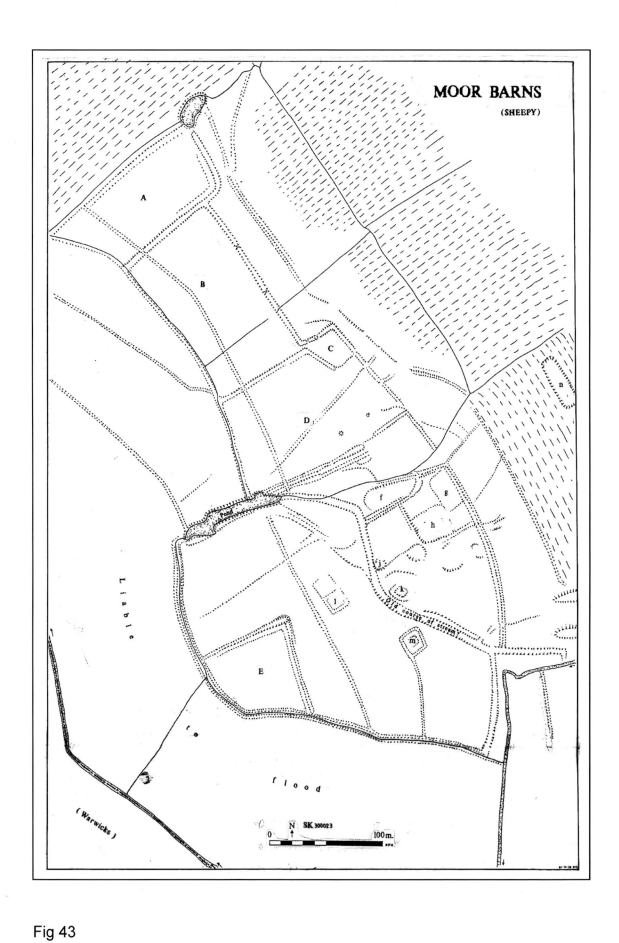

Fig 43

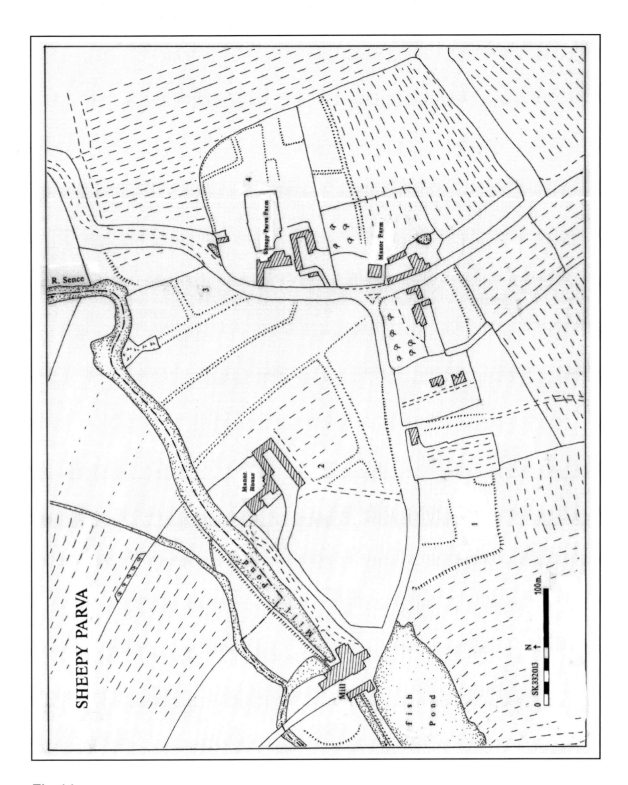

Fig 44

Sibson Village Earthworks(Fig 45)   SK351008

RAF vertical air photographs reveal earthwork evidence all around the small village of Sibson. There are traces of house sites and old enclosures at the west and east ends of the village, and opposite the Rectory. North of St. Botolph's Church were two substantial rectangular ponds, probably medieval or early post-medieval fish ponds, one of which appears on the OS First Edition map of 1885.

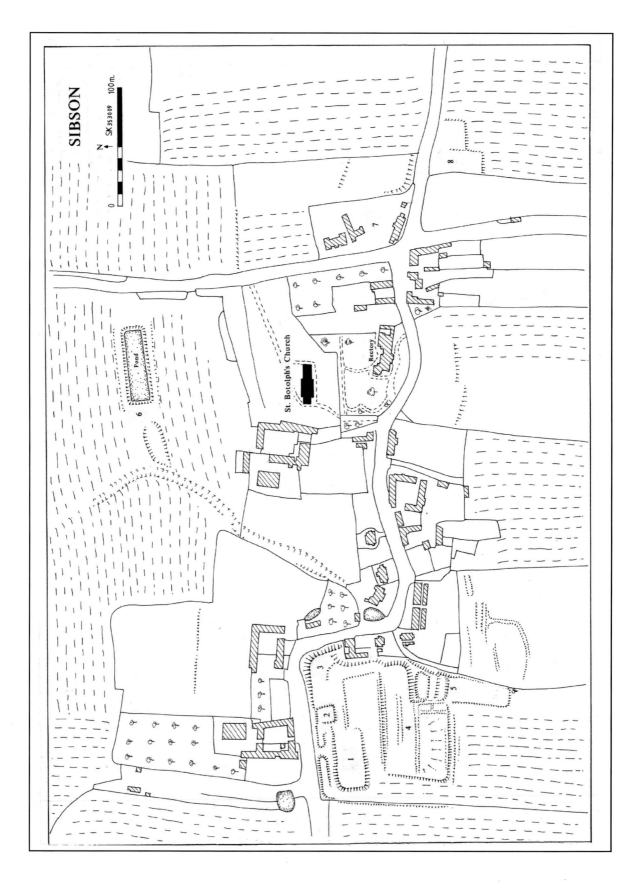

Fig 45

Wellesborough, Sibson, (Fig 46)   SK365024

This is a small hilltop settlement with evidence of earthworks formerly existing around the Manor House. To the south is an area (10 with earthwork evidence, enclosed on its south and east sides by a substantial ditch (a-a) and including possible sites of buildings (b,c,d,e). North of the Hall another area (2), long since ploughed, has revealed evidence of old enclosures and two possible building sites (f,g). There are other possible areas of former village to the west and to the north-east (3,4) and an intervening area (5) where any evidence has been destroyed by quarrying. Taken together these suggest the former existence of a substantial village. Depopulation has been reversed in the late 20th century by the development of Temple Hall and the NATSOPA Memorial Home, and by more recent infill.

Water Mills   SK356033, SK344024

Temple Mill (SK356033) and Sibson Mill (SK344024) occupy long-established sites on the River Sence. Temple has been considered a possible deserted village site, but there is no strong evidence of this.

STANTON UNDER BARDON

Village Earthworks, (Fig 47)   SK464100

In its modern form, Stanton is a linear village extending north-south, but earthwork evidence on RAF air photos (RAF 541:212, 8th Dec 1848) and a site visit c.1995, reveal that while this area includes an old enclosure (1) there was formerly more settlement to the west around Manor Farm (2), and west and south of the farm are traces of old enclosures (a,b). Another area to the north (c) is cut by a deep hollow probably made by clay digging to supply the nearby 19th century brickworks. Between Manor Farm and Main Street are traces of more old enclosures (d,e), and probable sites of buildings (f,g,h,j,k). Local information suggests a medieval chapel was in the vicinity of k. It was mentioned in the matriculus of 1120 and went out of use in the 17th century. An 18th century map (ROLLR Ma/301/2) confirms that there were two foci to the village, one on Main Street near the present school (SK466101) and one around Manor Farm extending eastwards to the T junction.

Horsepool Grange, (Fig 48)   SK470101

This was a moated grange farm of Leicester Abbey. It was granted after the Dissolution to Henry Grey, Duke of Suffolk. Nichols describes it as "formerly a considerable place, surrounded with moats." (Nichols J, 1811, p994).
At the time of the survey in c.1988 the house survived, surrounded by three sides of an overgrown and rubbish-filled moat. The First Edition Ordnance Survey map shows three ponds outside the moat (2,3,4). The area just west of the moat (5) has traces of subdivision by faint ditches, suggesting that it may have been a garden or orchard. To the north-west is another old enclosure (6) defined by banks (7,8). The stream appears to have been diverted to encircle the moated site.

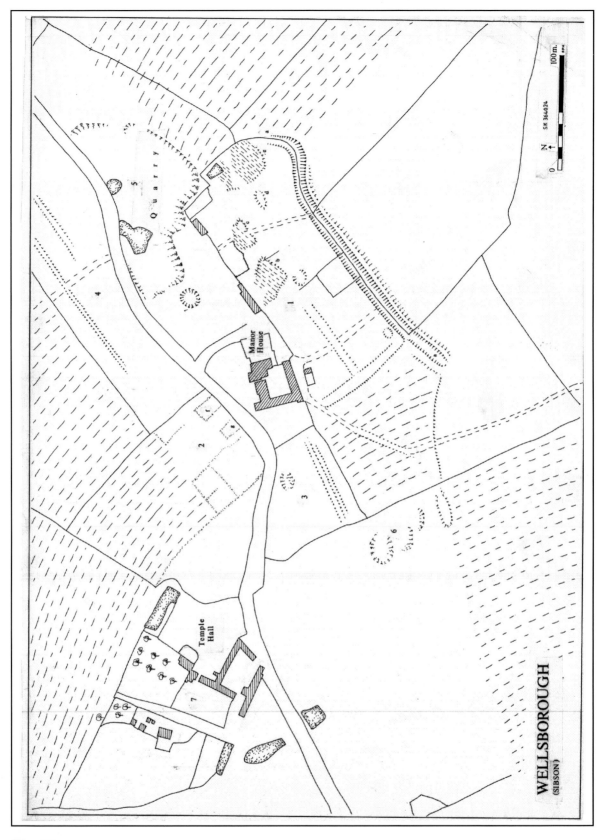

Fig 46

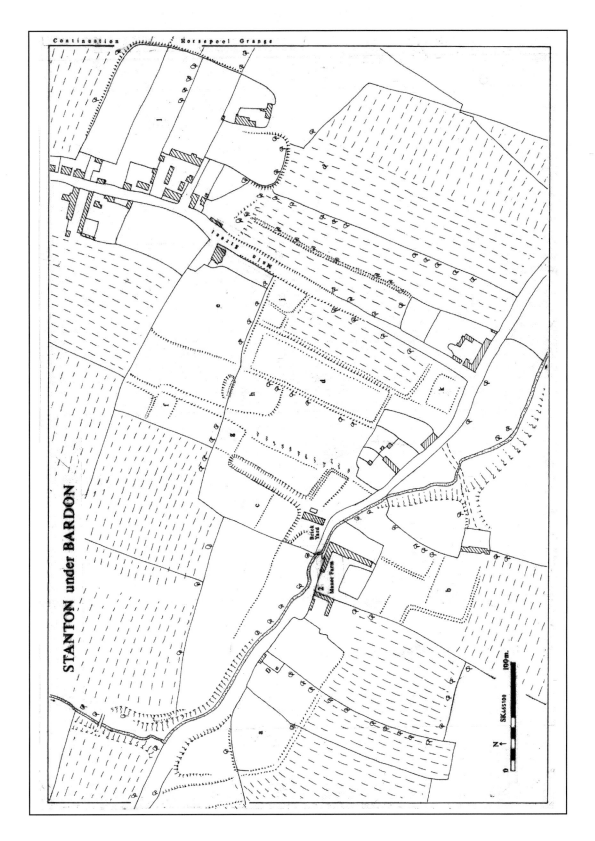

Fig 47

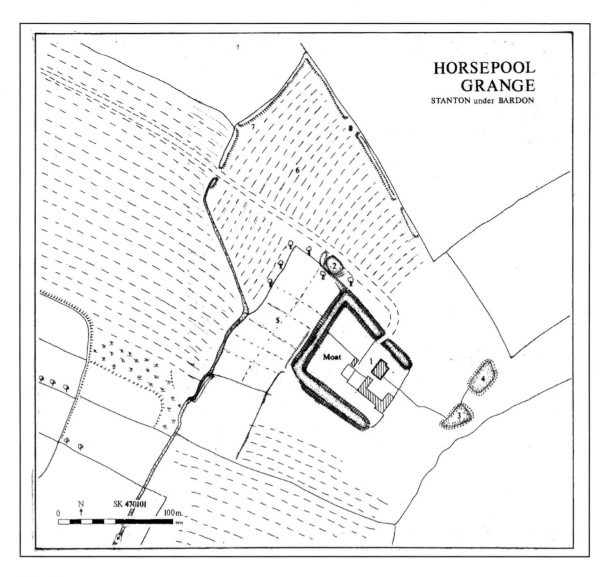

HORSEPOOL GRANGE
STANTON under BARDON

SK 470101

N

0   100 m.

Fig 48

STAPLETON

Village Earthworks   *SP434984*
There is an area of village earthworks just north of St. Martin's Church, including two house platforms and a hollow way.

Moats, (Fig 49)   *SP433988*
North-west of Manor Farm is a small rectangular moat, presumably the former site of the manor house. Aerial photographs taken by the RAF reveal that another, smaller moat and a fishpond (a) used to exist a few yards to the north-west, in an area partly enclosed by a bank (b). This smaller site might have enclosed a garden feature or a dovecote.

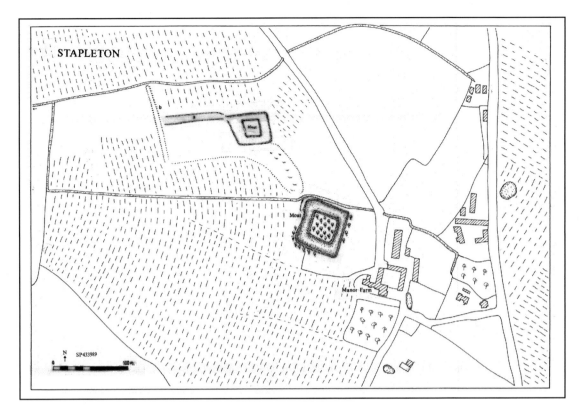

Fig 49

STOKE GOLDING

"The Moats", (fig 50)   *SP397969*

In the south-west corner of the village are earthwork remains of two fish ponds.
These are called "The Moats" and extend along the southern side of a field which
was called the "Park" on old maps. Within it are traces of the sites of old buildings
(a,b,c) and levelled terraces (d,e). This appears to be a fairly typical manorial garden
of the 16th or 17th century. North of the fishponds is a mound, apparently a prospect
mound. However its origins may be much older, as it was dug into many years ago
and part of an Anglo-Saxon hanging bowl was discovered (LCC HBSMR). 150
metres to the north is another mound, with the site of a summer house nearby,
indicating that there was a substantial garden in this area as well.

SUTTON CHENEY

Village Earthworks and Fishponds, (Fig 52)   *SK417003*

There are two areas of village earthworks recorded in Sutton, one being around St.
James's Church and the other around the old lane south of the Hall. In this part of the
village some ten buildings have disappeared since the time of the village enclosure
survey in 1797 (a,b,c,d,e,f,g,h,j,k,l), while others have gone near the cross roads to
the south-west.(Public Record Office MPL.39, copy in Leicester, Leicestershire and
Rutland Record Office). The earthwork evidence provides additional sites of
vanished buildings south of the church (1,2,3,4,5) and south of the Hall (6,7,8), where
at least four lanes used to meet (9). This is a good example of the way in which
cottages abandoned in the 19th century have left little evidence because the bricks
were taken away for re-use. In contrast cottages abandoned in earlier centuries,
although made largely of mud, have left more evidence because the sites were
simply left to grass over.

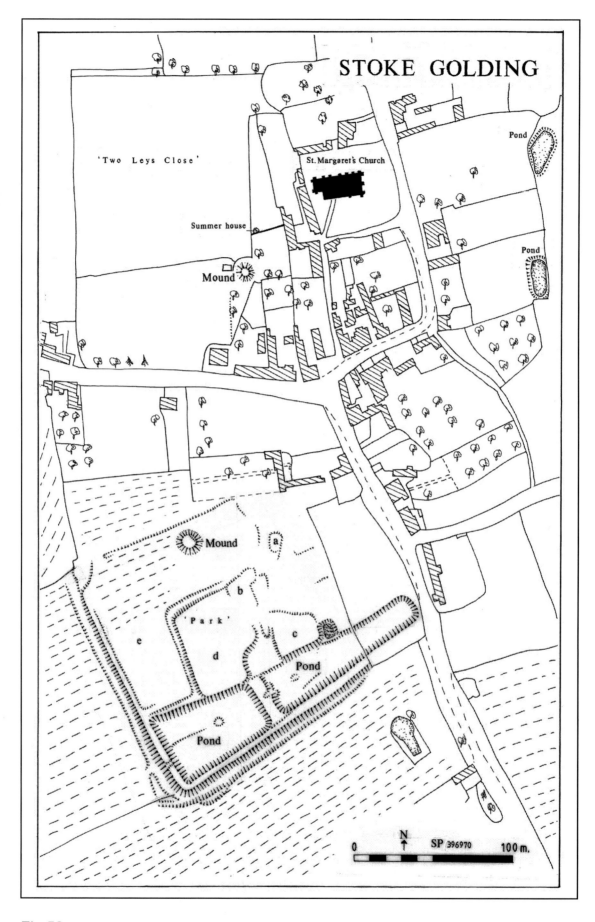

STOKE GOLDING

'Two Leys Close'

St. Margaret's Church

Summer house

Mound

Pond

Pond

Mound

a

b

'Park'

c

e

d

Pond

Pond

0   N   SP 396970   100 m.

Fig 50

The cottages south of the Hall were probably removed to allow the hall gardens to be laid out in the 16th or 17th centuries. There are garden terraces (10,12), a terrace walkway (11) and a fish pond (13). The village lies within a rectangular area defined by back lanes, three of which (14,15,16) survive as hollow ways.

Mounds   SK413006
North-west of the village are two earthwork mounds. One is in a ploughed field at SK414007, the other is in the garden of the old Vicarage at SK413006. The latter is well preserved and quite steep-sided, suggesting that it might be an 18th or 19th century garden feature. The former is a lower mound but situated on a ridge and is likely to represent the site of a medieval or post-medieval windmill.

Ambion Village, (fig 51)   SK400003
On Sunday August 21st 1485 King Richard III is said to have pitched camp on Ambion Hill on the night before the fateful Battle of Bosworth. The exact site of the battle is the subject of current archaeological research, but Ambion Hill has earthwork evidence of a village that was probably already deserted by the date of the battle. There are references to a small settlement here, the last being in 1346. There are slight earthwork remains just west of Ambion Farm, with probable house platforms (1,2,3,4,5,6) in an elongated rectangular area. To the south of these is a more-or-less square enclosure (7) within substantial ditches. This may have been an extension to the original village core.

In the 17th century this was called the manor of Anbein or Anebein, a lordship of 350 acres, and by the time of Nichols' survey it had long been entirely depopulated, but a farm was built here in the 19th century. The Battlefield Visitor Centre now uses the site. Just to the west is King Richard's Well with its stone monument. (Nichols J, 1811, p516).

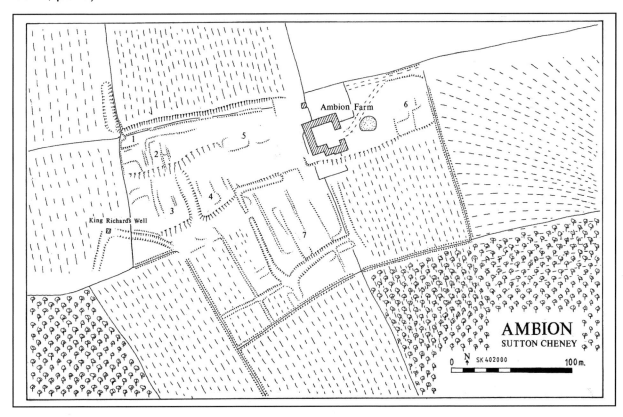

Fig 51

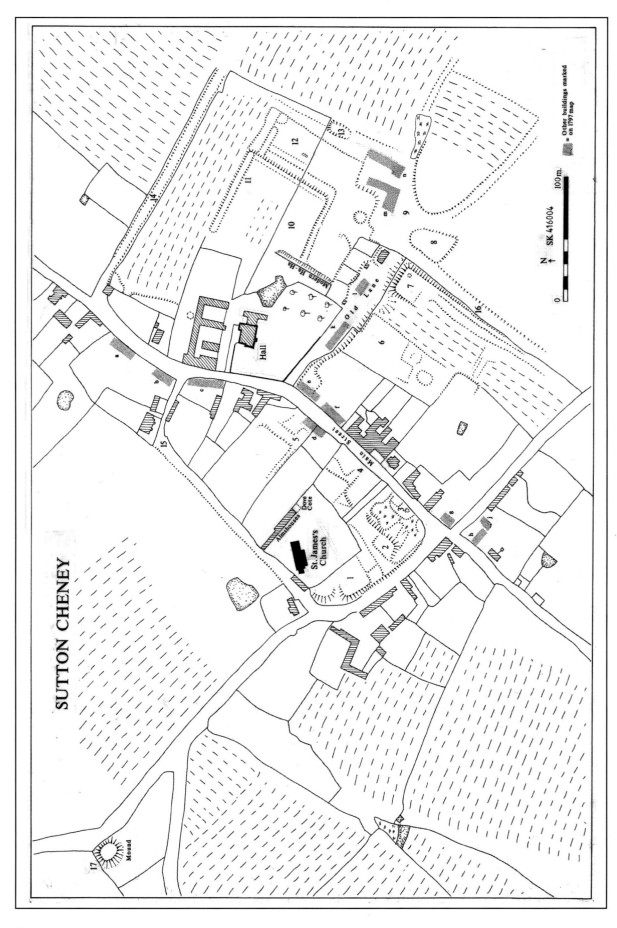

SUTTON CHENEY

St. James's Church

Almhouses

Dove Cote

Hall

Modern Ho-ho

Main Street

Old Lane

Mound

SK 416004

N

0   100 m.

= Other buildings marked
on 1797 map

Fig 52

66

THORNTON

Village Earthworks
SK468075,
SK462081

Thornton is now a continuous linear settlement, as a result of 20th century infill. However, the First Edition OS Maps, and an earlier map of 1794 (ROLLR Ma/322/1), show two separate nuclei. The first of these was around St. Peter's Church, and the second around the road junctions at the north end of the present village.
Both of these nuclei had 'back lanes' in hollow ways running along their western edges.

Water Mill
SK460078

Earthworks remain of the old mill race of Thornton Mill, marked as a flour mill on the 1885 Ordnance Survey.

TWYCROSS

Moat and Village Earthworks, (Fig 53)
SK337050

North-west of St. James's church is a well-preserved manorial site with a rectangular moat. South-east of it is an old enclosure with a fish pond, and to the north is a larger enclosure (1) subdivided by drainage ditches.
Along the northern boundary of this area are two more old fish ponds, parallel with the stream.

Taken together these represent a late medieval manorial site with a moated house, probably approached via a bridge and gatehouse on the south side. The enclosure to the east could have been a garden, whilst that to the north probably included orchards. Moat and ponds were linked by a network of water channels controlled by sluices.

West of the manorial site is a field (2) with at least three possible house platforms. To the north, across the stream, there were earthworks representing the former extent of the area of settlement called Little Twycross, with possible sites of buildings (3,4). These features appear clearly on RAF vertical air photos (RAF 541:212, 3092, 8th Dec, 1948) In addition there is evidence of the area of old sand pits, presumably dug in the post-medieval period.

UPTON

Village Earthworks
SP363996

There are several old ponds and slight village earthworks recorded around the hamlet of Upton.

WITHERLEY

Glebe terriers of 1679 record three open fields; Moor Field, Middle Field and Mythe Field.

Water mill
SP322976

Witherley mill was an old corn mill on the River Anker. The mill race still exists.

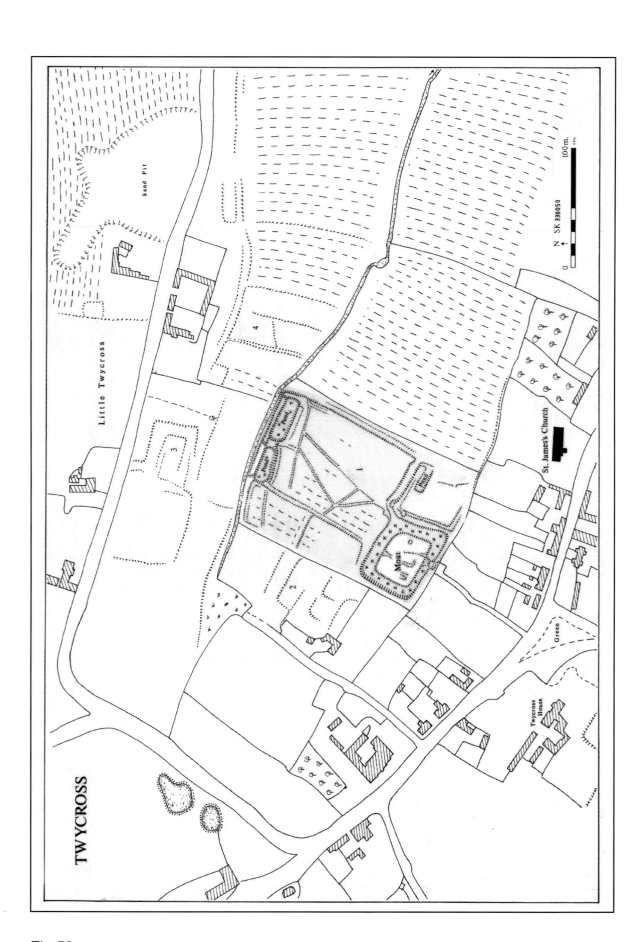

Fig 53

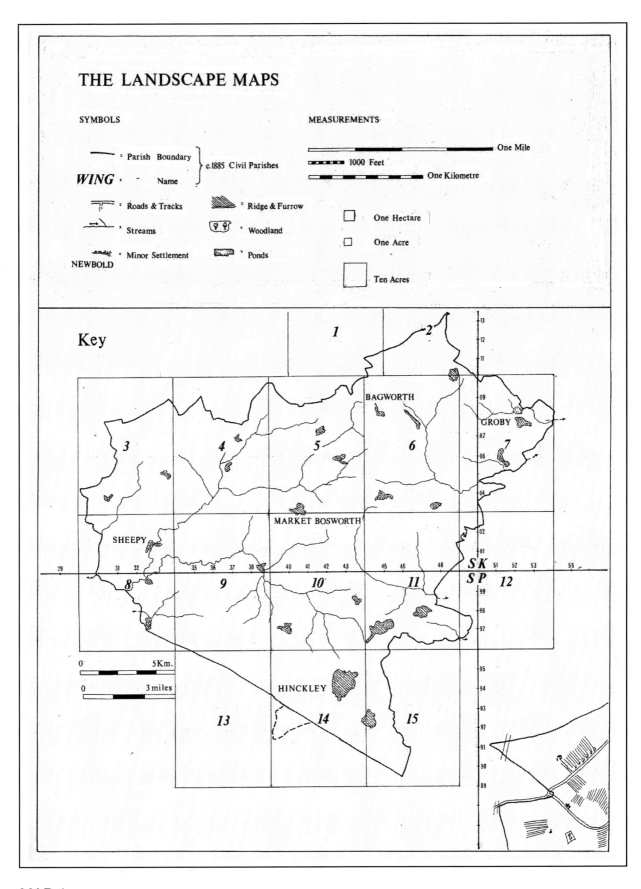

THE LANDSCAPE MAPS

SYMBOLS

— : Parish Boundary } c.1885 Civil Parishes
WING : Name

⊤ : Roads & Tracks
↝ : Streams
NEWBOLD : Minor Settlement

▨ : Ridge & Furrow
♀♀ : Woodland
▧ : Ponds

MEASUREMENTS

▭▬▭ One Mile
▭ 1000 Feet
▭▬▭ One Kilometre

□ One Hectare
□ One Acre
☐ Ten Acres

Key

1   2

BAGWORTH

GROBY

3   4   5   6   7

MARKET BOSWORTH

SHEEPY

SK
SP

8   9   10   11   12

0   5Km.
0   3 miles

HINCKLEY

13   14   15

MAP 1

69

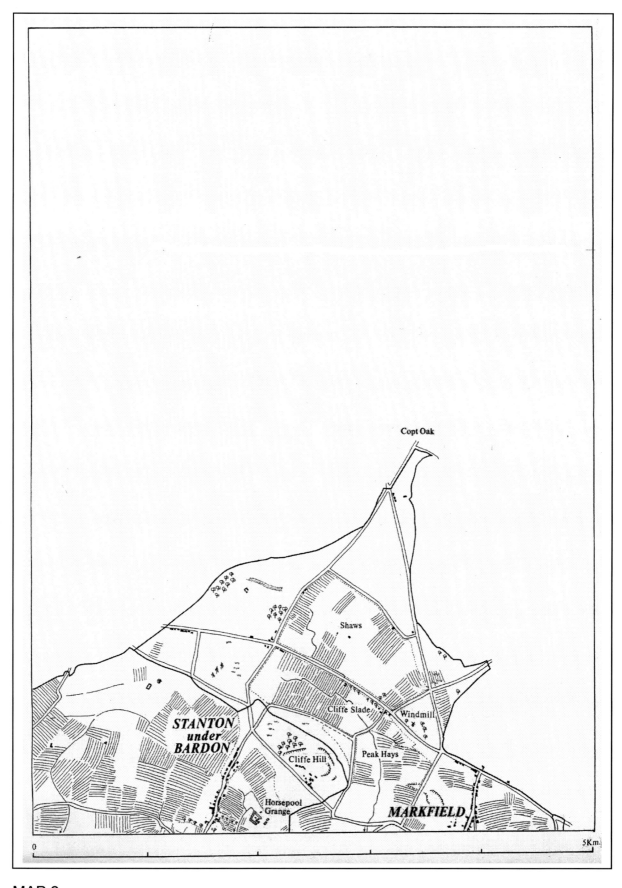

MAP 2

MAP 3

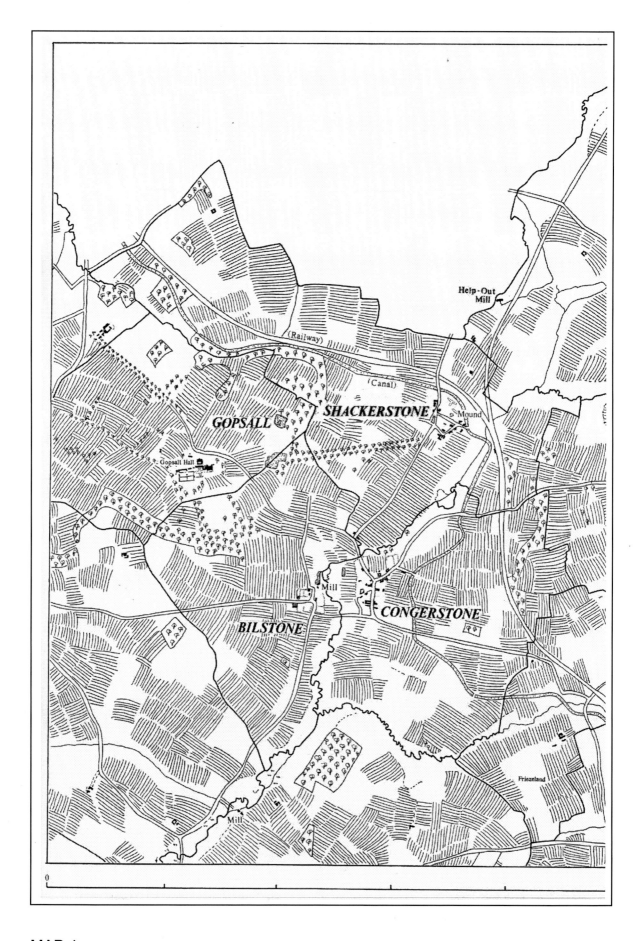

MAP 4

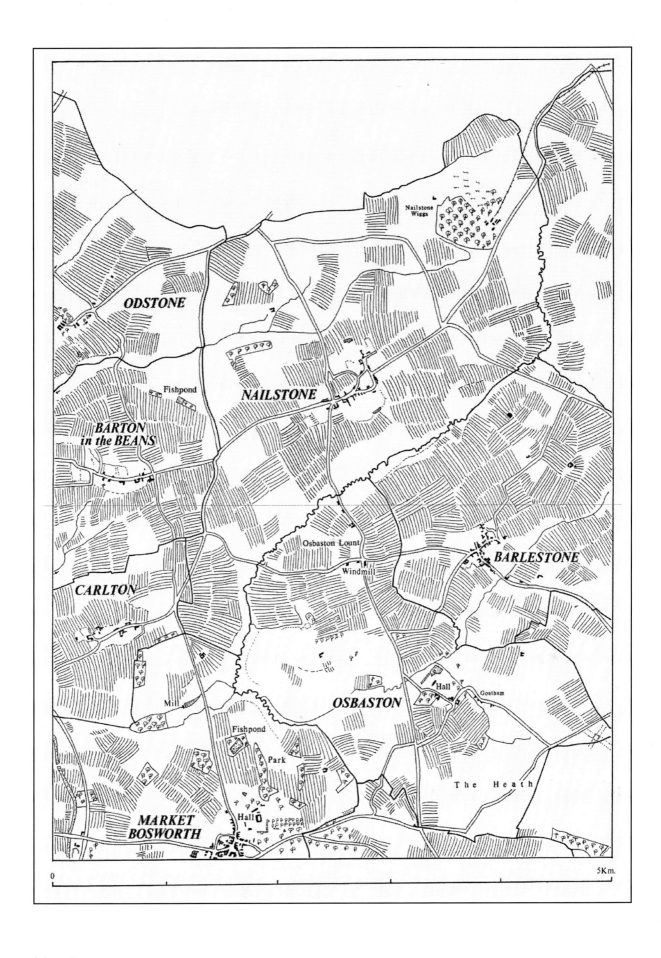

Map 5

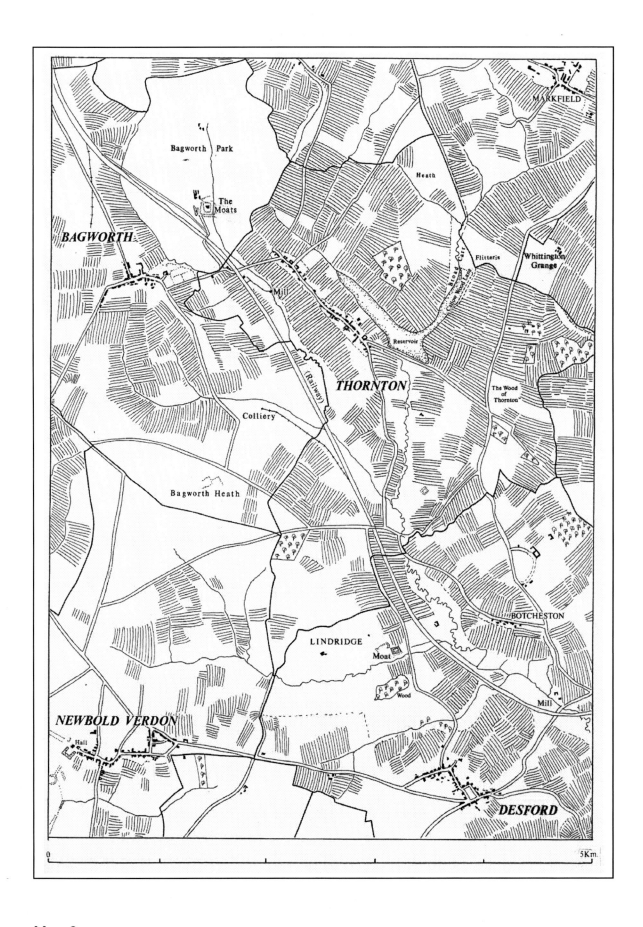

Map 6

74

Map 7

75

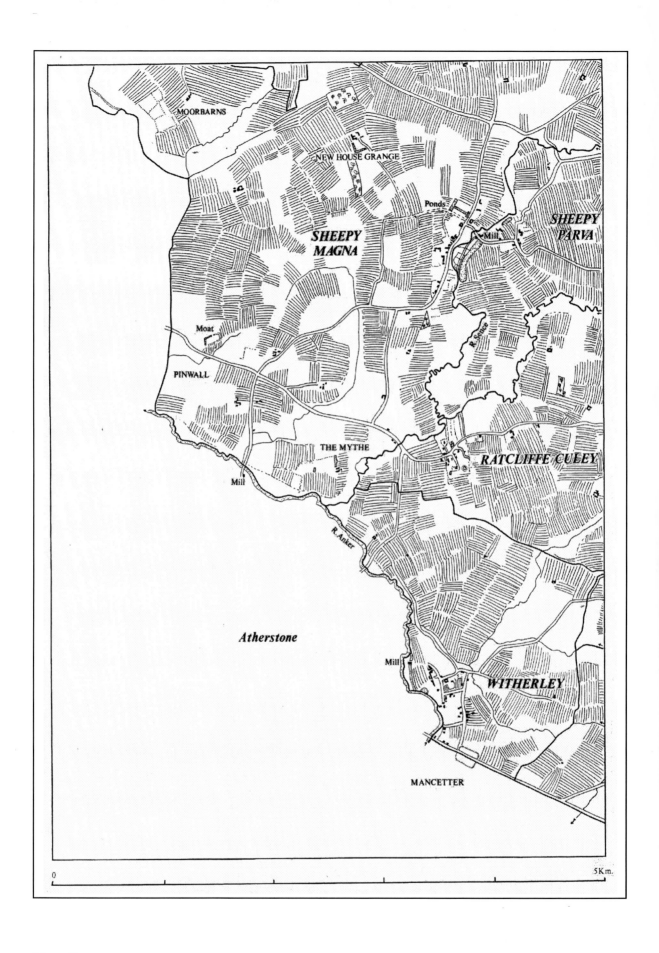

Map 8

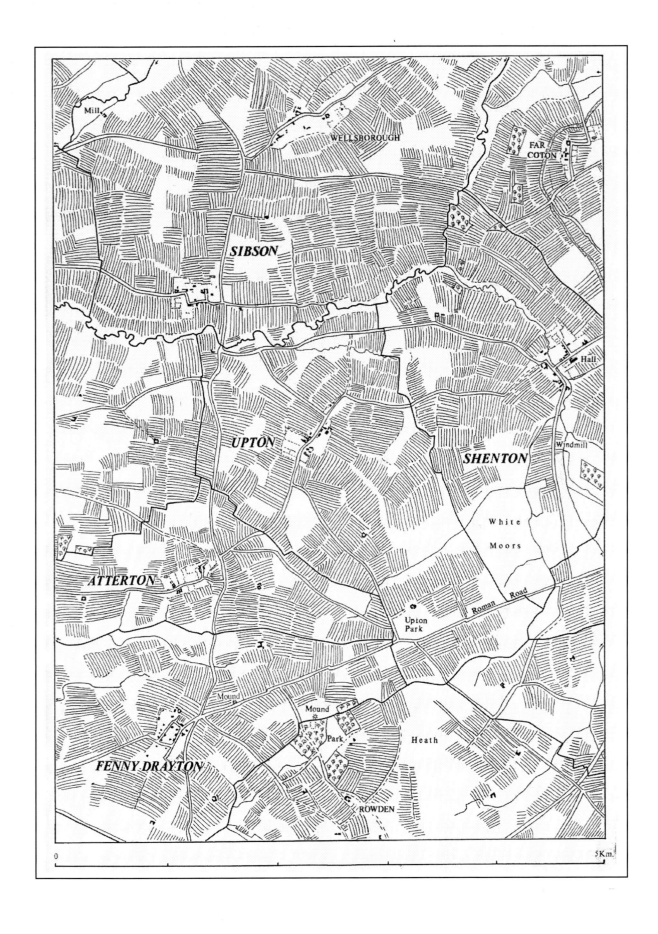

Map 9

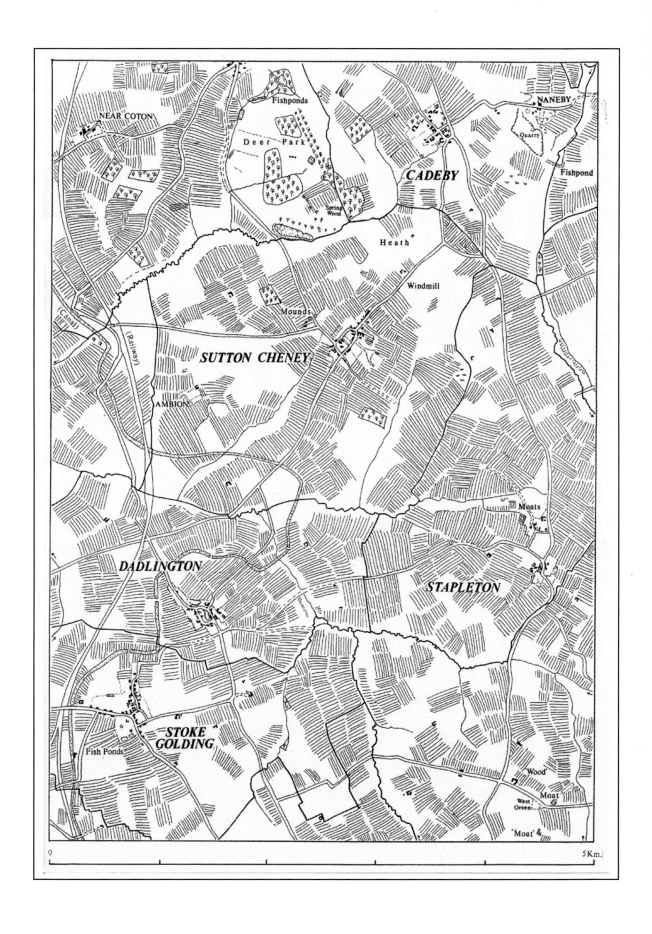

Map 10

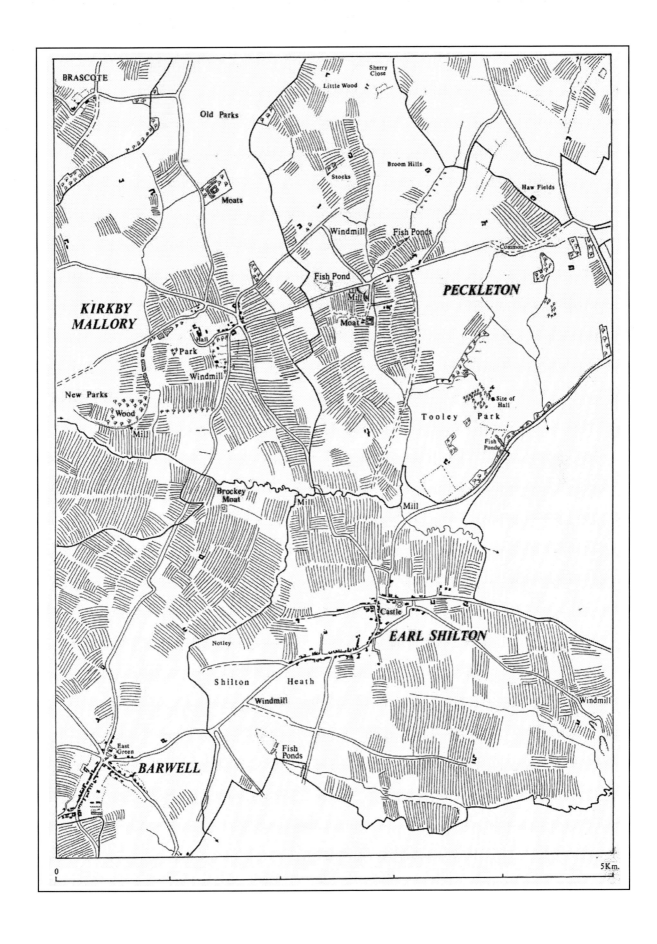

Map 11

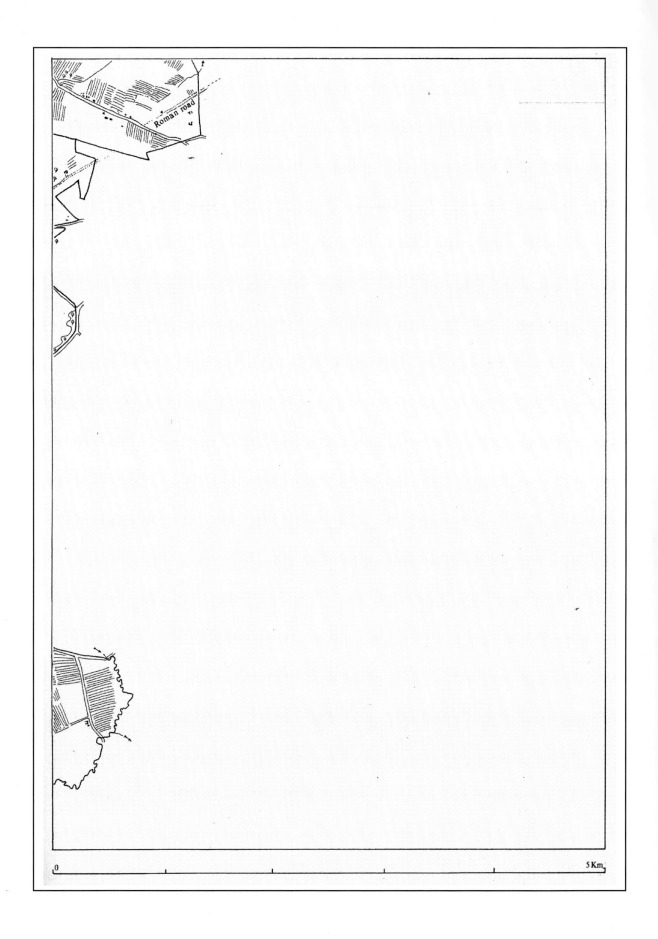

Map 12

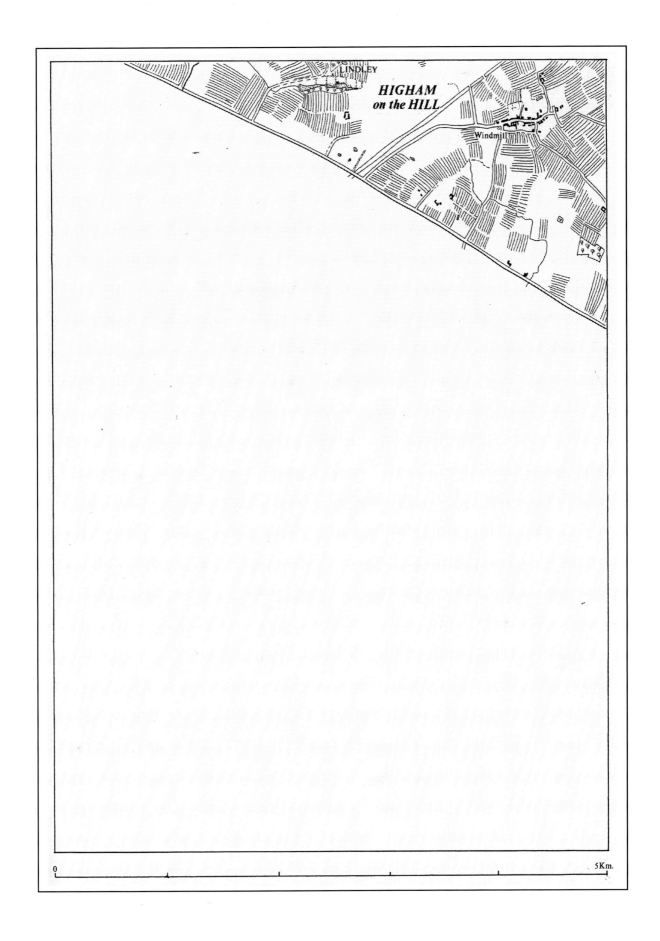

Map 13

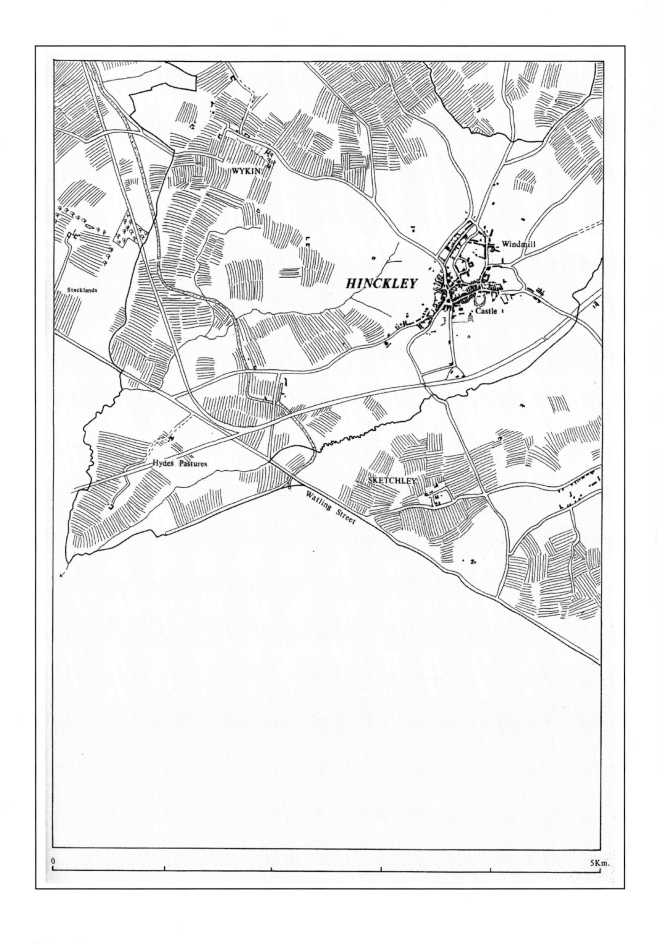

Map 14

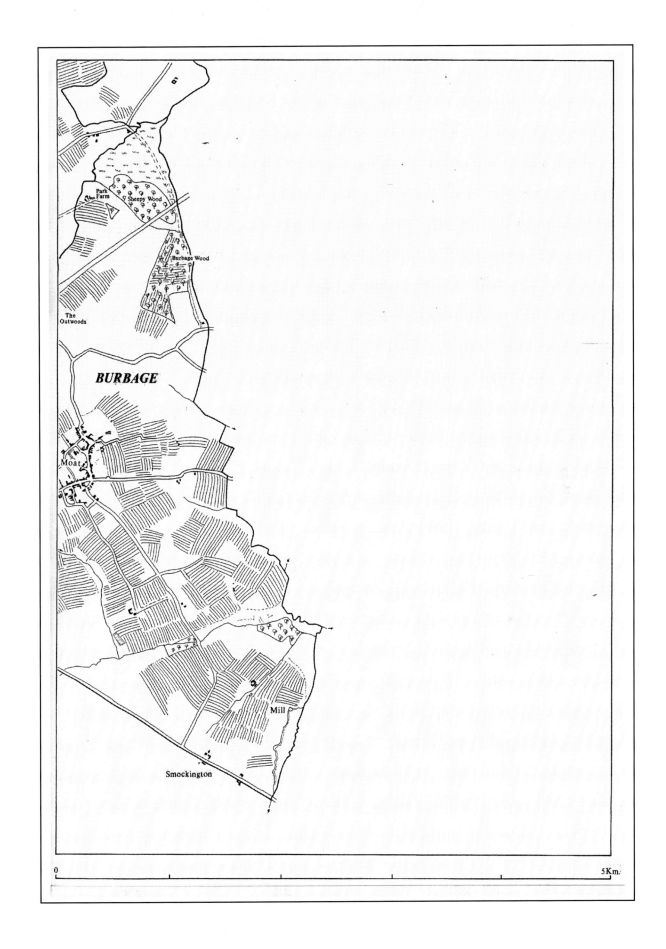

Park Farm

Sheepy Wood

Burbage Wood

The Outwoods

BURBAGE

Moat

Mill

Smockington

0   5Km.

Map 15

REFERENCES

Bloxham, M H, 1870, "Merevale Abbey" in Victoria County History of Warwickshire Vol. II, pp75-78

Cantor, Leonard & Squires, Anthony, 1997, "The Historic Parks & Gardens of Leicestershire and Rutland, Kairos Press, Newtown Linford, Leics.

Cantor, Leonard M, 1970-1, "The Medieval Parks of Leicestershire", Transactions of the Leicestershire Archaeological and Historical Society, Vol. 46, pp9-24

Cantor, Leonard M, 1977-8, "The Medieval Castles of Leicestershire, Transactions of the Leicestershire Archaeological and Historical Society, Vol. 53, pp 30-41

Cantor, L M, & Squires, A, 1997, "The Historic Parks and Gardens of Leicestershire and Rutland", Kairos Press, Newtown Linford, Leics

Courtney, Paul, 1977, "The Monastic Granges of Leicestershire", BSc Dissertation for Dept. of Archaeology, University College, Cardiff. Published in 1981 in Transactions of the Leicestershire Archaeological and Historical Society, Vol 56, pp33 – 45.

Creighton, Oliver, 1997, "Early Leicestershire Castles: Archaeology and Landscape History" Transactions of the Leicestershire Archaeological and Historical Society, Vol 71, pp21 – 36.

Crocker, J, 1981, ed "Charnwood Forest, A Changing Landscape" Loughborough Naturalists Club, Sycamore Press, Wymondham.

David, Carol, 1989, "Vegetarian History and Pollen Recruitment in lowland lake catchment: Groby Pool, Leicestershire", Loughborough University of Technology Dept of Geography Working Paper Number 4.

Farnham, G F, 1933, "Leicestershire Medieval Village Notes", 6 Vols, Privately printed, p132

Foss, Peter, 1983"The History of Market Bosworth", Sycamore Press, Wymondham.

Fox, Levi & Russell, Percy, 1948, "Leicester Forest", Edgar Backus, Leicester.

Hartley, Robert F, 1984 "The Medieval Earthworks of North-West Leicestershire" Leicestershire Museums, Arts & Records Service, Leicester.

Hartley, Robert F, 1989 "The Medieval Earthworks of South-West Leicestershire" Leicestershire Museums, Arts & Records Service, Leicester.

Hartley, Robert F, 1989, "The Medieval Earthworks of Central Leicestershire" Leicestershire Museums, Arts & Records Service, Leicester.

Hextall, Keith B, 2002 "Know Your Barlestone: The History of a Leicestershire Village", Barlestone and Osbaston Community Association, 2003 2nd edition.

Hoskins, W G, 1942-3, "The Deserted Villages of Leicestershire", Transactions of the Leicestershire Archaeological and Historical Society, Vol 22, p242

Liddle, Peter, 1982, "Leicestershire Archaeology-The Present State of Knowledge" Vol 2. Leicestershire Museums, Arts & Records Service, Leicester, 1982.

Nichols John, 1811, "The History and Antiquities of the County of Leicester, Vol. IV pt II, Sparkenhoe Hundred." By John Nichols, London. Republished by Leicestershire Library Service in 1971 in association with SR Publishers Ltd. Other volumes are occasionally completely referenced in the text.

Oakley, Glynis, 1996, "A History of Gopsall", Barncroft Printing.

Pevsner N, 1960, "The Buildings of England – Leicestershire", London, 1960.

Ramsey, David, 1995, "The Location Puzzle of the Old Groby Mill" , in Leicestershire Archaeological and Historical Society publication The Leicestershire Historian No. 41.

Squires, A & Humphrey, W, 1986 "The Medieval Parks of Charnwood Forest", Sycamore Press, Wymondham, Leics.

Squires, Anthony, 1995, "A Provisional List of the Medieval Woodlands of Leicestershire (excluding Rutland) c1200 – c1530", Transactions of the Leicestershire Archaeological and Historical Society, Vol 69, pp86-96

White, W, 1846, "History, Gazetteer and Directory of Leicestershire", Sheffield, p536

Archaeological Reports in TLAHS

Clarke, David T-D, 1952, "Archaeology in Leicestershire 1939 – 1951", Transactions of the Leicestershire Archaeological and Historical Society, (Brockey Farm Medieval Coffins/picture), Vol 28, pp40-41

Liddle, Peter, 1979-80, "Reports of Fieldwork 1980" in "Archaeology in Leicestershire & Rutland 1980" (Barlestone Manor House pottery), Transactions of the Leicestershire Archaeological and Historical Society, Vol 55, p95

Meek, James, 1996, "Archaeology in Leicestershire & Rutland 1995, Sketchley Hall, Sketchley Old Village, Burbage", Transactions of the Leicestershire Archaeological and Historical Society, Vol 70, p158, compiled by Richard Pollard and John Lucas

Gossip, James, 1996, "Archaeology in Leicestershire & Rutland 1995, Kirkby House Farm, Kirkby Mallory", Transactions of the Leicestershire Archaeological and Historical Society, Vol 70, p159, compiled by Richard Pollard and John Lucas

ULAS, 1999, "Archaeology in Leicestershire & Rutland 1998", Cadeby animal bones, Transactions of the Leicestershire Archaeological and Historical Society, Vol 73, p86